CHEAP MOVIE
TRICKS

CHEAP MOVIE TRICKS

How to Shoot a Short
Film for Under $2,000

By Rickey Bird

CORAL GABLES

Published by Mango Publishing Group, a division of Mango Media Inc.

Cover Design: Rickey Bird
Layout & Design: Roberto Nunez

For permission requests, please contact the publisher at:

Mango Publishing Group
2850 Douglas Road, 2nd Floor
Coral Gables, FL 33134 USA
info@mango.bz

For special orders, quantity sales, course adoptions and corporate sales, please email the publisher at sales@mango.bz. For trade and wholesale sales, please contact Ingram Publisher Services at customer.service@ingramcontent.com or +1.800.509.4887.

Cheap Movie Tricks: How to Shoot a Film for Less Than $2,000

Library of Congress Control Number: 2017906610
ISBN: (paperback) 978-1-63353-543-5, (ebook) 978-1-63353-544-2
BISAC category code PER004010 PERFORMING ARTS / Film & Video / Direction & Production

Printed in the United States of America

Dedicated to the strongest woman I know

Anita Catherine Vivo-Williams

I love you always Grammy

TABLE OF CONTENTS

Introduction to
Short Films

BIG TRICKS,
SMALL PACKAGES

Hey, you, with the camera. Yeah, you—the aspiring filmmaker. We've been watching you, trying to get your attention for a while now. Want to know something?

We believe in you.

That's right. You probably didn't realize this, but we know you're a little lost right now, not knowing how to use that camera, attempting to figure out what kind of story to tell, planning a budget (that you don't have) for set, makeup, actors, editing, sound and light. You've really created an unreachable fantasy. Anyway, listen up. You *can* make quality indie short films. You really can.

For starters, you need to *get your butt off the couch*. Uh oh. You're not on the couch? You're locked in a closet? You're actually sitting in the dark thinking your movie dreams might be over? Is it that bad? Stop this nonsense.

Quit crying about not having a $25,000 budget for that short film you always wanted to make about two psycho lovers, or the one about that zombie who can live without his head while wandering aimlessly through Hollywood searching for it. You don't need that much money to pull it off. And no more whining. A film school degree is not the only thing that will help you hone those indie filmmaking skills you desperately need to grow.

Got your attention now? Good. Listen. No aspiring filmmaker requires $25,000 to make a short film. And, a film school degree isn't what makes your moviemaking skills shine. It's *you*. You have to put in time and learning. You have to work hard. You have to figure out how to frame scenes, how to direct, how to edit, how to organize, how to cut corners...

You have to cut lots of corners.

In fact, by following the directions we've prepared in this book, you can learn how to make solid short films that you can show off at film festivals. Oh, and guess what? You can do this without a film degree or deep pockets. Along with some inner drive, some moviemaking gear, some money, and a lot of ingenuity, you can get really far in the film business.

So, yes, we're on to you. We know what you want. You bought *Cheap Movie Tricks: How to Shoot a Short Film for Under $2,000* because you need to make short films so bad your eyeballs are starting to burn. You want some help. *Admit it.* You want a self-help book for moviemakers. Something that will take the sting out of those flaming eyeballs. Can't say we blame you with the catchy title and the sheer awesomeness this book has to offer.

Here we are. Just what you've been looking for, ready to help mold you into a smart indie filmmaker, a cost-cutting planner, a genius storyteller, a creative editor and filmmaking effects guru. Seriously, before you know it, all your friends and a whole lot of strangers will think you're some kind of magician. *Alakazam!*

You'll have us to thank, because *Cheap Movie Tricks* is less expensive than film school and a lot easier to swallow than that giant budget you don't have. Who can afford that crap anyway?

But hold on. There's something you should know about being a filmmaker. Before we can even get started we need to be in agreement. About what, you ask? About the fact that filmmaking isn't an easy process. There's just no easy way through this career path. Better go sell paper dolls or make mud pies for a living if you want something mindless to do with your oodles of creative energy. If you really want to be a filmmaker, you must solemnly swear to stay committed, to be incredibly focused. Above all, you must have a positive outlook no matter what.

Got all that? Not in the closet anymore? Are you on your feet? Good. Dust yourself off. Dance around with this book in your hands. Go ahead. We're excited, too! That's because you're about to start learning how to take the short film process from the beginning of a project all the way to the film festival circuit. It's a long road, but not as long as you think. And if we can do it, you can, too.

Here's what you need to do. Think of *Cheap Movie Tricks* as a reference guide to help you have a better understanding of all indie filmmaking processes. You'll learn tips about locations, story and script, budgets, sets, costumes, talent, crew, special effects, makeup, filming and editing tricks, sound and light, promotion, and the film festival circuit.

Did we mention *Cheap Movie Tricks* is about to blow your mind? You're probably already saying, "Where the hell has this book been my whole life? Why didn't I give these guys a hundred bucks for all these great ideas?"

Don't worry about it. Just follow us on all those fancy social media sites and we'll call it even.

•••

Wait a minute. Is that doubt we see creeping across your face again? Now you want to know whether you should even make short films if you have this book with so many great filmmaking secrets!

So why short films?

Simple answer: Short films are a constructive way to get *you* into the film industry. A solid short film is a stepping stone, one that will grant you the potential to get noticed by producers willing to fund your next film (short or feature length). Of course there's a caveat. Your work has to be good. Maybe even great. It will take more than a few tries. That's another reason you don't want to start with a feature film. You don't want to invest all kinds of money, time, talent, etc. into a film, and then afterwards suddenly realize, "I should have started smaller, much smaller. My skills aren't up to speed. What was I doing when I emptied my bank account into a film I can't sell?"

The short film process helps you hone your craft and works your filmmaker muscles in ways you can't imagine. Learning the process on a small scale turns your creativity into a focused lens rather than a sloppy mess. Let's say you want to build houses. You build a small model of a home to show people that you can actually build a house. They like your architectural style. They say you're great at it. They want you to start building houses. *Think about it.* If you didn't take the time to make that model home they might not have hired you. Now, instead of a model home, we need to see what you're capable of doing with filmmaking on a smaller, more manageable scale. Get it?

BIG TRICKS, SMALL PACKAGES.

You might even get a career out of it.

One more thing before we really start focusing on *Cheap Movie Tricks*. You know the idiots who say not to spend time making short films? They usually have a ton of money. A lot of them went to film school, possess oodles of natural talent, and can shoot a feature on Daddy's dime. So what? Not everyone has the same opportunity.

How about the guy who made *Avatar*? Self-taught. Tarantino and all his flicks? Self-taught. Or maybe Robert Rodriguez—who now owns a whole TV network and shoots big-budget Hollywood movies from his house? Self-taught. Look, the biggest mistake filmmakers often make is taking advice from people who have no idea what the hell they're talking about. So please, *spend a lot of time on short films.* But start with *Cheap Movie Tricks*, because by the end of this book, you'll be a filmmaker! Now, grab your camera, and as Samuel L. Jackson says in *Jurassic Park*: "Hold onto your butts!"

Figuring out your short film end-goal

If you want to be featured in a particular film festival, start researching to see what works and doesn't work for that festival's fan base. Tailor-making a film for a festival, or even for a certain industry, will help you get on your way. Want to get into the horror film industry? Start researching horror festivals now. You never know who you will meet. Some short films at festivals are getting produced into features. Remember, short films can be artistic statements, or they can act as resumes for the film industry. Sometimes they do both! Figuring out the end-goal of your project will help steer you in the right direction.

Getting ready! Short film checklist

CAMERA

If you don't have a camera, you don't have a movie. We recommend using a DSLR camera. They look like they only take pictures. Surprise! DSLRs do video, too! You should be able to get a nice Canon with a decent zoom lens for around $500.

LIGHTS

Lights make or break the film quality. You have several options. Most hardware stores carry bell lights. They look like big silver bells with a clamp on the back. These lights are the easiest type because you can clip them anywhere. Cost: under $10.

BELL LIGHT

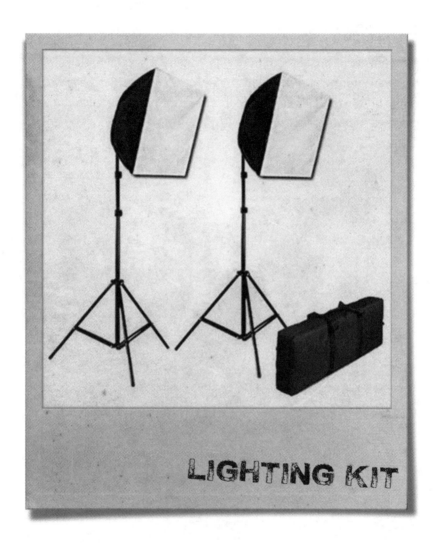

SOUND

If movie sound sucks, so does the movie. Do not use the mic on the DSLR you just bought. Always record sound separately. There are some inexpensive sound-recording devices that capture high-quality sound. We like Zoom recorders. Cost: around $100.

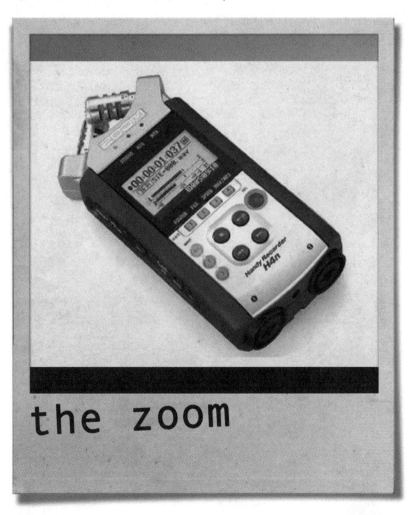

the zoom

Short films made into indie features

Short films showcase your talent. It's a good idea to keep a full-length feature idea handy when putting together your script. Think we're kidding? *Saw*, *Sling Blade*, and *Napoleon Dynamite* were all short films. Maybe you already have a feature idea. Even better. Pull some elements from the feature you're thinking about and make a short film.

Chapter One

STARTING YOUR FILM PROJECT

The Location Situation

Aha! You thought it was the script that came first. Not in low-budget cinema. Locations, or as we say in the film biz, *LOCATIONS!* (screamed like a mythological siren) are the first elements you should think of when filmmaking on a micro-budget. Remember, locations are those places where you film actors, record all their cool lines, and sometimes create sets. They're the backdrop for your characters, are part of your story, and add crucial texture to your scenes. Here at Hectic Films we insist on finding cheap locations, or better yet, *free locations*. Seriously, we know you don't have a budget for actors besides the five McDonalds cheeseburgers you promised. So what makes you think you're going to have boatloads of cash to spend on that beach scene in Maui? Yeah, scratch that fantasy.

Locations can make or break your project. Filming a scene in your Aunt Judy's yellow-stained bathroom she never cleans might not work for a tale of middle class Americans with a housekeeper. That fight scene you planned in a garage full of taxidermy squirrels? Might not be a good choice for what was supposed to be the private quarters of a nuclear scientist. Oh, and that treeless park no one goes to down the street? Bad idea for your personal remake of *The Blair Witch Project*. It's supposed to take place in a forest, remember? Not to mention, the police can shut you down, fine you, or even make arrests if you have fake weapons and/or no permits. Maybe this is a good time to remind you that you and your crew need to dress like filmmakers. We prefer to wear our Hectic Films shirts with pride while on location. Quiet on the set!

All right, enough of that. Let's talk about what kind of locations you should be searching for. Get out your map, your car (or your friend's bike), and start checking out potential locales in your area. First, you need a location where you can shoot one or more scenes. Somewhere you know you can always film without being bothered by nosy people (for the record: don't be mean, just tell anyone curious about what you're doing—that you're working hard filming a masterpiece).

Location examples include locally-owned businesses, downtown alleys, halls for rent, parks (be careful not to get in trouble or set up in a park that will be crowded by nine in the morning), cheap motel rooms (make sure to check for any pre-existing crime scenes—unless that's part of your film, then SCORE! Just kidding. If you see blood, call the cops and run away). If you don't have money or access anywhere (come on, be creative, surely there's someplace available) then you can use your home. That's free, right? You'd be surprised how many scenes we filmed at city structures then finished all the interior shots in our own homes.

We know what you're thinking. *How can there still be a cost if the location is free?* As Hectic Film's Rickey Bird's Grandpa always says, "Ain't nothing for free."

Remember throughout your film journey—even free stuff costs.

For example: a gas station in another town says you can film on location this Saturday. Super cool. Now factor in travel costs for your film crew and actors. Gas, food, even lodging will sneak up if you don't plan well. Another example is using a forest or park. Sure, those may be free, but have you thought how you will get electricity for lights? Trust us, you always need lights. What about having too many locations? Yes, you can have too many. That's time and money. Think about it. Pack up your film gear, ship out to your location, unpack, film, repeat. No thanks.

All right, moving along. You've found a location. Your buddy says you can use his apartment to film something, anything. Great! Now what do you do? You give your friend a huge hug. Yes. No! There's more. You need reference photos. You might not even have an idea, let alone a script. Right now you just want to see what you have to work with. Now, go to your friend's apartment and photograph each room to later use for references as you write your story (a.k.a. future script). The beauty in this day and age is you can use your smart phone to store pictures of your locations. Snap photos as if you were framing for the film. Be precise. This is for your movie. Pretend you're watching a scene unfold. Two people arguing. Frame and snap. People eating food and talking about the end of the world. Frame and snap. Repeat throughout with every idea you can think of. Once you write your script you can come back and take more photos if needed. Remember, photos of potential scene locations will help your team get on board with your project. You'll get your ideas across better. So, snap away!

STORYBOARD FROM INFERNUM
BY CRAIG FRASER

Uh oh. You forgot to ask an important question. When is the apartment available? Can't go over there during the Super Bowl or during your buddy's epic all-night *Dungeons & Dragons* campaigns. Finally, you set up filming dates. Don't forget *pick-up shot* dates too. Those are the shots that filmmakers always realize they need after the fact. Trust us, filmmaking is sometimes all about imagining new scenes, close-ups, or long-shots. By the way, grab yourself a glossary of film terms. You're gonna need it.

A lot to think about already? None to worry. Take a breath. This is a good time to slow down, ask yourself a few quick questions about your location...

If I'm filming at a structure, what's the natural lighting like inside and out?

Which direction does the sun come up in relation to the exterior of the location?

Hey, when filming either during day or night, you have to think about how light changes on the interior (buildings have windows, duh) or the exterior of our locations.

See how the light shinning through changes the look of the scene?

THIS SIDE
TOWARD SCREEN

This is where your photography skills come in. They'll be important when it comes to composition and lighting. Smart lighting makes films visually interesting.

By the way, we recommend shooting indoors as much as you can while on a micro-budget. That's because *you* can control the lighting. Outdoors, you can't control the sun, clouds, rain, or dust storms, as well as all the curious onlookers and nosepickers who might arrive (along with the cops if stealing a shot). This quote by Alfred Hitchcock sums up shooting anything outside: "In feature films the director is God; in documentary films God is the director." Seriously, it applies.

Last but not least! Check out the bathroom status at your locations and make some notes so you can tell your crew. Trust us, bathrooms are very important. Note the toilet paper amount as well, or everyone on your set could have a really crappy time.

When all is said and done, if you're working with a business, city government, county agency or individual, it's time to take out your *Location Agreement Form* (we'll talk about contracts later). Have them sign the form before you do any work at that location. You'll need to sign it, too.

Congratulations! You officially have a location.

CLEANLINESS

Don't be a dirtbag. Clean up after yourself as you film your movie. You don't want to damage a location or leave it a wreck. If you don't keep your location clean, you also increase the chance of losing equipment. At one location, someone chucked our tripod mount because it got placed near some trash. Yeah, it has happened.

LOCATION SAFETY

Safety first! Devise a quick safety plan in case of fire, earthquake, meteors, space invaders... You get it. Just come up with a head count system to keep track of everyone on set. Include a meeting location where everyone should go in case of an emergency. You also want to have the nearest hospital location and phone number. One last thing: keep a medical kit on set at all times. Include extra Band-Aids and tissues for hurt feelings...

LOCATION OWNER ISSUES

If your location owner wants to be there during filming, then let them. Show them how grateful you are for them allowing you to use their space. Remember to show you care about their property. Remember to be respectful of their stuff. Bring some cleaning supplies and clean up after yourself. This will really help when you need to do crucial pick-up shots at that location. Otherwise they may say, "See ya later. Film somewhere else."

PLAN B

We recommend securing a back-up location. In the world of indie filmmaking, nothing ever goes exactly as planned. NOTHING.

DON'T GET ARRESTED

The real trick is to not get arrested. You think we're kidding? Here's a story. One night a few moons ago Hectic Films was filming a shooting scene for an indie feature. We were in a downtown bar and had permission from the owners. Of course the cops showed up. They were being sneaky. *Really sneaky.* They waited outside, hoping to nail us on some trumped up charge. But as Rickey left to walk up the steps, he was greeted by three cops with guns out. Someone had seen us in the bar with guns, didn't know we were filming, and called the cops. Once they were alerted that we were shooting a film, they left us there to finish our scene... Indie Filmmakers 1, Cops 0. Of course, we've seen less careful film teams arrested for stealing on-the-go shots. One group of filmmakers was shooting scenes in a parking garage. No permission. Easily seen from the street. Easy access for cops to bust everyone involved, make arrests, and take their fake guns; they weren't able to finish filming their project. *Tsk, tsk.* Cops 1, Indie Filmmakers 0. Let this be a reminder that guns are a huge no-no when filming in a public space. If your character has a gun, then re-write your public scenes so your character doesn't use or display a weapon. No guns, folks. No one wants to actually get shot. Please remember, you and your small crew will be the only ones who know the guns are fake. Don't bring real guns on set and respect the police when they come onto set.

PUBLIC SPACES

Parks, bus stops, parking garages, even crowds may help your project—and usually require permits. It's tough to get good audio in them, but they're great for montage or flashback scenes—pretty much any type of scene that doesn't require audio and can be replaced with music and or voice over. You didn't hear this from us, but if you're low key, then who's to say people can't think you were filming some home video while in a public space? *Escape From Tomorrow* was entirely filmed at different Disneyland parks with handheld cameras and incognito actors reading scripts off their phones. Ever see *Lost in Translation*? Some of the scenes in the street crowds were shots totally stolen by Sofia Coppola's film crew. No way could they have afforded that with their budget. Our favorite story is about when Alfred Hitchcock stole a shot of the United Nations building with Cary Grant in *North by Northwest* after the UN told him he wasn't allowed to film there. We're not telling you to break the law. But don't get caught. And don't blame *us* if you do.

Some of our favorite location cheats

It's a good idea to get *extra location shots* while filming on location.

Imagine yourself on a scavenger hunt for gold. This "gold" is the really cool images you're seeking for your film. The shots can be of anything. For example: if you see a fountain in front of the cheap motel where you're filming, grab a couple of shots. Why not? You might use the footage as an establishing shot of some kind. Maybe the footage will appear in the film for some completely unknown reason! That's golden!

Here's another location cheat: right after filming a close-up dialogue scene with your actors, don't move your camera. Have the actors leave the frame, then record ten to twenty seconds of "clean slate." Why? This way you can use a green screen later for any pick-up shots. You never know. You might have another scene you want to film, or worse—maybe something went completely wrong with what you already filmed. Either way, once you have that clean slate footage, you've saved yourself from having to drive to get that shot again.

Chapter Two

STORIES THAT DON'T SUCK

Story 101

I t's time to discuss storytelling. Not scripts. Not yet. That's the next chapter. Don't you dare jump ahead. We need to talk about *story*.

That's right—the basics. Call it *Story 101*, a brief lesson so you don't get confused. Consider this a warm-up, a way to get to know your inner writer self. When you do sit down to write a script, you want to have some idea of direction, where to look inside yourself for that wonderful story you're going to tell (even if it is about a Halloween clown hell bent on prank calling radio stations while torturing some poor victim. Oh yeah, we did that one). Okay, enough of that. Let's get down to science!

Writer Lisa Cron says something remarkable about our DNA. She says our brains are wired for story, that our blabbing to each other about our lives is an inherent human condition. She writes in *Wired for Story*: "Our brain developed a way to consciously navigate information so that, provided we have the time, we can decide on our own what to do next. *Story*." She says storytelling is something our brains do naturally and implicitly. She quotes neuroscientist Antonio Damacio who tells us, "It should be no surprise that it [storytelling] pervades the entire fabric of human societies and cultures."

Yeah? So what? What's he talking about? It means that when the boss isn't in the office we all sit around someone's cubicle sharing tales. It's our default mode.

It means *you're a storyteller*.

We're all storytellers.

It's what we do.

Story brain science is in our DNA.

"We think in story," writes Cron. "It's hardwired into our brain. It's how we make strategic sense of the otherwise overwhelming world around us."

And that's good. Especially if you think, "Oh man, I have to go to school to learn how to tell a story."

Nahhhh.

Think about it. Your BF calls. She's *all* about the drama in her life. She tells you a few stories. Guys do this, too. Hell, *everyone* gets a little dramatic now and then. We share politics, history, who got murdered, and *how*, or why that local politician is taking bribes, who hates you, and who likely wants you dead (because they unfriended you on social media. Not us, we swear!). And don't forget all that reminiscing about the time you ran away from a herd of wild poisonous pigs and *survived*.

We tell stories. It's what we do.

In a way, we've already defined what story means—something that's told or revealed. We can also say a story is an account of something that's happened, or is happening before our eyes. Newscasters like to tell stories in real time if they can find a juicy car chase or dramatic shooting filmed from helicopters high above the scene. Radio announcers do the same thing. Ever hear the way they dramatically call a game in real time?

Stories can be about the past, present, or future. Every TV show, film, novel, memoir, short story, poem, history book, diary, text message is a form of story. Those forms can be experimental, like a novel written with hidden notes, or a film like *Boyhood* shot over twelve years. Did you see that one? *Boyhood* was a part of writer-director Richard Linklater's DNA. He conceived of the 2014 film way back in the nineties. It was eating at him. "It happened in stages," he told *Time* in 2014. "I felt like I wanted to tell a story about childhood. I had been a parent for a while..." So, it just came out of him as he was doing what people do, raising kids, being a dad. Awesome!

There was a real risk for him to tell the story he was somehow wired to tell. That's because the film was such a huge experiment. No one had written a story like that before. Piecemeal over more than a decade and shot little by little as the actors aged. Was the story told that way because of his storyteller DNA? Starting to see how knowing you're wired for story can help you as a filmmaker? Those urges in you grab you. They want you to be creative, and they want you to tell stories that come from a natural place in your core. This is incredible to know! Even if your story is about an alien octopus that time travels!

But what makes a story worth telling? You share an account of Cousin Larry who works in a county office of boring cubicle dwellers. As it unravels, you desperately want your audience to be riveted to the story. You tell it as if you were there. You explain all the harrowing details. You're *that* dramatic. The last thing you want is to be boring, but everyone walks away, because, well, in hindsight, you only told a story about a boring office worker checking his email while the boss isn't around. Good luck keeping anyone awake with that riveting tale of corporate nothingness. Couldn't Larry have at least gotten fired by email?

You have to have plot. You have to have style. Take Tarantino for example. When *GQ* interviewed him about how his film idea for *The Hateful Eight* creatively emerged, he was already building on a past project, *Django Unchained*. He told the magazine in a December 2015 article:

I liked the idea of creating a new pop-culture, folkloric hero character that I created with *Django,* that I think's gonna last for a long time. And I think as the generations go on and everything, you know, my hope is it can be a rite of passage for black fathers and their sons. Like, when are they old enough to watch *Django Unchained*? And when they get old enough—14 or 15 or something like that—then maybe it's something that they do with their fathers, and it's a cool thing. And then Django becomes their cowboy hero. And so I like the idea of maybe like a series of paperbacks coming out, *Further Adventures of Django,* and so I was really kind of into that idea. And then I started writing it as a book, as prose. And that's what ended up turning into *The Hateful Eight.*

Wow! Multiple layers of stories! Tarantino had some real motivation behind *The Hateful Eight*! It was a novel that was a sequel to a film where he wanted to create pop-culture heroes for kids to share with their dads! He was wired for story and found an awesome connection! A real meaningful one! Take that Cousin Larry!

In comparison, the story about Cousin Larry just isn't riveting. It doesn't even come from a good place. Those kinds of story wires are crossed. They leave everyone unfulfilled. They don't come from the core of you. They're just lip service without meaning. Re-read what Tarantino said to *GQ*. Why was he writing? He had something to say! And he wanted to really affect people for a long time.

Here's another example of *boringus americanus*:

You think you're a wiz because you thought up this great story about an American family. A dad who works at a bank. A wife who stays at home. And two children. So you start writing, imagining the tale unfold. The story opens with the father being late for work. The mother argues with her kids who need to head off to school. The mother feels stressed. So does the father. End of opening scene.

What's wrong with that? Everyone arguing and late for work and school? "Wasn't that tension-filled?" you ask.

Um, no. BORING. SNOOZEFEST. FLATLINE. LAMESAUCE. Wake us up in the afterlife. You just captured every single boring account of American life all wrapped into one.

Why isn't that story riveting?

It's far too common. Meaning, there's nothing unique about it. We all know it and live it. On top of that, *nothing happens*.

Going to work or to school isn't a story. It's as bad as telling the story of the teenage boy watching videos on YouTube. People stare. So what? BORING.

When you're wired for story, you have to find some kind of meaning, one that's unique, one that connects with people and makes them want to know what happens next. We all know what happens in the boring story about American life. Kids go to school. Parents go to work. Snooze.

So once again, everyone walks away while you're telling your snore-worthy account of the most boring family on the planet. Doesn't even matter how dramatic you tell it. Now throw your brain onto hot coals. Watch the grey matter bubble and cook. Trust us. It will be more exciting than your Cousin Larry and stressed family tales.

Okay. Before you pop your lid, let's see if we can salvage anything here.

How about a Godzilla shows up to the next cubicle while Cousin Larry's checking his email? Godzilla, who is talking real fast, just landed this telemarketing job and doesn't want to come off wrong when explaining to people how to login to their new fancy computer tablets. And since Cousin Larry's just been fired over email, all hell is about to break loose because he's about to tell Godzilla to shut up. Yup. Yup. Conflict. Tension. And, in that other story about the family, what if while the parents are arguing, the TV news shows a meteor hurtling toward earth? And what if—at the same time—the dad has found out his best friend is part of the scientific conspiracy to hide the idea that the meteor can be destroyed? Yep.

Suddenly the stakes are upped. The audience is interested in the motivation. They want to know why the family is acting normal when they might be about to die. Do they not see the meteor on the TV? Do they know about the impending obliteration of everything and don't care? Why is the son wearing an "I Love Meteor Day" t-shirt? Now everyone wants to know what happens next! They want to know the motivations of the characters in the cubicle, too. Why does Godzilla need this job? Who is the co-worker? Why is she staring at her monitor? Does she really hate Godzilla as much as Cousin Larry? Maybe he took the job of her former lover. There's some resentment going on, folks. This is story! You're wired to tell it!

Now we need some character and scene development. Most of all, your audience needs to know what every character wants. Let's look at some fictitious situations. Cousin Larry wants his job back. Godzilla wants to be loved by *anyone*. Only, you're not going to give these pesky characters what they want. You're going to torment your characters, and that, friends, will torment your audience. That's what we call *Cheap Movie Trick*'s first holy commandment of storytelling: *never give a character what he or she wants.*

Just don't do it. As bad as you want characters to win... Don't let them. This kind of conflict and tension will keep your audience riveted. They will want to know the outcome. Godzilla wants that first telemarketing call to go smoothly. Don't let it. Another co-worker wants to make friends with the scaly monster. Don't let it go smoothly. You want the family to notice the television when the meteor is hurtling. This is yours for the taking. Build the tension. Make your audience squirm.

Are there exceptions to our holy commandment of storytelling? Maybe. But don't you think you should follow our advice for a while to see how your story develops without all kinds of happy little rainbows? Forget rainbows! Harry Potter has a scar on his head day one and never gets what he wants. He can't even make a potion right.

Let's take this further. Riveting stories, the ones that make you turn pages or keep Netflix streaming, have the uncanny ability to really get into the main character's head. This is easier in prose. You can write what a character is thinking, how Jennifer wants to toss her guts because she's terrified of what the judge might say if she's caught not just holding up a liquor store but sleeping with the judge's son, who happens to be a cop. Now dive further, go past specific character thoughts into character feelings. You can describe all sorts of emotions. Make them desperate. Painful. Jarring. Stomach churning. Tortuous. Good job.

In film, feelings and thoughts have to be conveyed through solid acting (and voiceover and other devices, too). We want to feel when we write the story because we want our characters to feel. We want to go on an emotional rollercoaster because we all want an exhilarating emotional experience. You don't always have to add a meteor or a Godzilla. But remember, exhilarating emotional experiences don't come from stories that regurgitate the most humdrum parts of our lives. They come from when we up the stakes and the emotional pain.

Write a story you'd want to hear, or read, or see. That will make the entire process a little more meaningful for you as you put pen to paper before you even get to the script.

Oh, and one more thing. Remember what we said about location? Don't forget to write a story that fits your locations. We'll remind you again when we talk about scripts.

BTS from "Descensus"

What's a scene?

A scene is the primary element of your reader's powerful emotional experience as you present them with your story. The cause and effect of scene structure has three basic parts:

1. *Goals*. What the heck do your characters want or need to do?
2. *Obstacles*. This is the tension and conflict that causes your story to keep going because your character fails to reach the goal(s).
3. *No Victory*. If every chapter ends in victory your reader will fall asleep. Keep the stakes high. Keep the tension off the chart. Make your scenes full. Give them a beginning, middle, and end. If they don't have *goals, obstacles, no victory*, or a *beginning, middle. and end*, then your scene is not fully developed.

Scene dialogue that works

Remember, in dialogue, characters need to banter. They need to argue over wanting something and shouldn't be granted any sort of victory. We keep the tension high that way. Meet John and Jennifer. Jennifer wants an apple. John wants Jennifer. Neither reaches their goals in this mini scene. Observe how they ask questions yet receive no answer. If an apple can cause tension in a scene, imagine what else you can do as a writer and filmmaker.

EXAMPLE: APPLE SCENE

John has a red delicious apple. He takes a bite.

Jennifer wants it. She sits on the edge of his desk. "I love apples. Doesn't matter what kind. Granny Smith, Fuji, reds..."

John's not buying it. His stomach hurts thinking about where she might have been. "Where were you last night when I went to the store?"

"I just love them." She watches him chew. "Everything about the crispness, the taste."

"You were supposed to go with me," he says. "Where were you?"

"Just cut off a little piece for me," she whines. "Doesn't have to be big."

John takes another bite. "You were with Peter, weren't you? I don't like that guy. Never did. You know he did something to Jesse Garner. Everyone knows it. Everyone except the cops."

"Why does it matter where I was?"

John swallows, holds out the apple. "You want this? Tell me where you were, why you stood me up. Then we'll talk about apples."

Action moments we're proud of

Most storytellers will say the story isn't in the action—that action is an easy way out. "I can't think up a good ending, so how 'bout I blow everything up!" Okay, that's an extreme example, but the fact is, we *love* action. We integrate as much as we can. Let's face it—action will probably help you get attention with your short film. What constitutes action? Someone running. Good. Someone fighting. Even better. Find some stunt actors who need to build a demo reel and suddenly you have more options! Let's face it: great stunts, car chases, shootouts, and zombie attacks are pretty cool. Did we mention we love action? Here are a few action moments in Hectic Films movies:

1. *Explosions:* They're dangerous. Use CGI only. Either way, sometimes they look cheesy, kinda like in the movie we worked on called *The Lackey.* Even we think we showed too many booms. Sometimes an explosion can be as simple as pointing away from the scene and shaking the camera, then adding some noise sound effects.
2. *Cutting up zombies!* We sliced a few undead in *Naked Zombie Girl* with a trusty fake chainsaw. During a screening at Screamfest, folks watching the crazy action stood up and started clapping. Action speaks louder than words, right? (More movie magic on zombie splatters later).
3. *Gunfights.* We emptied our rifles in the mini-Western *Mable.* We think shootouts are great for just about any kind of film. Audiences perk up when bullets fly.

What makes a well-developed character?

Ah, our second holy commandment of storytelling: *Characters feel everything.* Well-developed characters don't require fancy clothes and a lightning bolt scar when you're coming up with one to base your story around. Give your character desperation and emotion. Develop that. Let the rest of the story tell itself.

Horror story moments in our films

You know the feelings of terror you want your actors to convey in a good horror scene? That's why scream queens have to be really good. They reveal that moment of sheer terror that we all want to safely feel when watching a horror flick. Here are a few scenes in our work where we strove to capture that feeling of fright.

1. *Familiar Spirit* uses what we like to call the *demon cam.* During a ritual in the film, a spirit floats down the street into the house and possesses its victim. Frightening!
2. *The Deadlines* builds up a murderous character in the film by telling tales of him throughout. When he finally comes on screen, you're already frightened. Gahhhh!
3. In the middle of a zombie takeover, we stripped *Naked Zombie Girl*'s main character of everything, even her clothes. We did finally give her a chainsaw. Don't worry Mom, she wasn't really naked. Prosthetics literally covered every family jewel.

Writing in various mediums will help you as a Screenwriter

Nicholas Belardes writes in just about every genre imaginable. He swears that learning how to be a poet (not a rhymer—there's a difference) can truly help you with language. But you have to study poetry, learn the craft. He writes essays, too. He tells lots of personal stories in his book *Ranting Out Loud: Life, Pop Culture & How We Sometimes Don't Get Along.* His short stories are highly accessible and online at various journals. Think about it: short film/short stories.

Might be helpful for you to read some. Better yet, try your hand. Dig in. It will help your creativity. You can find links to these four stories on nicholasbelardes.com:

- *St. Augustine the Starfighter*: a monkey tale about child cruelty.
- *The Middle of the Passage*: two sisters on an island have a car that only drives backwards.
- *Gaspar*: A tough Hispanic kid learns a life lesson about tolerance and intolerance.
- *A Different Kind of Boiling Point*: An aged labor leader holds a secret about her youth.

Chapter Three

NO ROOM FOR CRAPPY SCRIPTS

Writing Films That Fit Your Budget

C hecklist time. You have your location. *Check.* You're gung-ho about making a short film. *Duh.* You understand what a good story is. *Check.* You have a screenwriting program to write your script. "Uh oh," you say. "I wrote all my story notes on napkins and toilet paper."

Hell yeah! That's a good start; means you're being creative. Bonus DIY points. Who cares what you wrote your story on? Write it on your forehead for all we care. Oh, wait a minute. Your entire film crew and all the actors need a copy. And the story you wrote based on the locations you acquired needs to be in script form. Crud. Better write a screenplay.

All right, let's jump right into the cheap-ass budget method of creating your script.

First off, if you don't have a computer, steal one. *Just kidding.* Borrow one when no one is looking. *Again, joking.* It's 2017. You don't have a computer? What the hell?

Seriously, the best way to write a script is by using a screenwriting program, and the best type of screenwriting program is the one that says *free* next to it.

Some filmmakers say there's a certain screenwriting program that must be used in order to be a professional filmmaker (not naming names or program names—why would we do that?). Either way, not true in indie filmmaking. And to be real, we just don't see a difference when you have a printed PDF of your script in front of you. Our experts have gone over these scripts with mega-magnifying glasses and chemically tested them in our secret laboratories. They came up with no differences!

We recommend Celtx (this can change. Do your research!). It's free and we believe the program functions close to industry standards. We're not forcing it on you. Feel free to browse the Interwebs and grab another free program. We just go with what already works.

All right. Got that cousin's computer you promised to borrow for only a week? And some Internet? (Hopefully that's free, too.)

Great. You're almost ready to start typing your script.

Screenwriting *used to* require intensive formatting. Back in the olden days, you had to be Albert Einstein to know all the indents and fancy tabs. You had to input those yourself into a word-processing program. Forget about it. Those days are over. Nowadays, screenwriting programs do this for you. Aren't you lucky? Pat yourself on the back. Technology loves you.

Before you think we're going to hold your hand through every filmmaking glossary term imaginable, think again. How does it go?

Let us *Google* that for you? Seriously, look up and familiarize yourself with script terminology. Screenwriting programs even help with scene headers these days and have lots of tutorials and help functions. You'll be toggling between DAY/NIGHT/CONT (the time of day your story is taking place) and INT/EXT (interior or exterior scenes) and CHARACTERS with ease. Before you know it, you'll be zooming through your script, fleshing out scenes, writing engaging dialogue, descriptions, and within a few days (if not sooner), you'll have a rough draft.

But don't think you're done writing.

Nope.

Now comes the part most beginning writers hate: *critiques*.

Sometimes called workshopping your script, critiques are when you take your rough draft to some serious writers who know story, plot, visuals, characters, etc. Warning: do not share your script with your mom who works for county wastewater. Nor share with your wife who sells cars. Forget family. Well, not totally. Wait, yes, forget them. They'll ruin you. Hold on now. Don't get mad. Think about it. You need some artists in your life, some fellow filmmakers, some writers who understand the creative process. Don't take your script to people who aren't artists. They won't know what they're talking about. Ask them to support your filmmaking career in other ways, like helping out at screenings, or donating money for equipment and acting talent. Don't have them read your script. Never the script. Not even if they beg. Yes, yes, there are exceptions (once every 10,000 generations), but do keep this in mind—non-creative types will say the most vile things imaginable. We can just hear some teen-horror filmmaker's mother throwing a script, screaming, "Why do you want to make a movie about chopping someone's head off? Your father and I thought we raised you better than that!"

"It's about orcs, Mom. Killer orcs. In a mythical land."

"No, it's about you wanting to kill everyone."

BLAH BLAH BLAH.

Back to your script.

Set your ego aside. Really. Dislodge from your five-star ego brain for five seconds. Every story and script needs revision. No first draft is amazing (though the ideas behind them may be). It's your second, third, or sometimes your fiftieth draft that shines. Is the script in your friends' hands? Good. Your filmmaker and writer buddies will understand how your story needs to match your locations. They'll see whether or not your dialogue is too longwinded, or too boring, or too choppy. They'll catch those underdeveloped scenes and flat characters, and help you identify those areas that could grow your story.

These are called developmental suggestions. And do us a favor. Don't just ask your buddies if they like your script. Does your ego really need a pat on the back? You can say that crap to yourself in a mirror. And don't ask your friends *yes* or *no* questions. Allow them to write detailed suggestions.

Does this mean your pals are right about everything?

No. This is your story. Your script. And most of all, *your film*. Their suggestions are just that. Suggestions.

You make the critique changes that you feel works. But set your ego aside. Don't make excuses for your characters. "Well, Sebastian really is longwinded, so-o-o..."

RIGHT.

Make the changes.

You'll grow this way. You do want to grow into a decent filmmaker, don't you? Well alrighty then. Write the first draft, get it critiqued, and then revise that baby. Do the process again, especially if there are still areas that you don't feel great about.

Now, here are some other screenwriting tips...

when Rickey gets left
alone on set with
prop money...

KNOW YOUR BUDGET

So you want to make a short film about a space battle involving ten thousand actors, five hundred space vessels, and seven hundred robot soldiers?

Since when are you Ms. Moneybags? Or Mr. Goldbuns? Have you forgotten already that this is a short film on a budget of $2,000? Pizza alone for your crew and actors will literally eat up that budget. Okay, you've gone temporarily insane. We understand. You're excited. You want to make a movie. You forgot that movies are about feelings, about people, about transforming lives. For a minute there you thought movies were about transformers, wars in stars, treks in stars, and orcs fighting hobbits while on the backs of gargantuan dragons. You forgot that you need to learn the art of human interaction, that two people talking in conflict, no matter what the costumes are, is a pretty tough act. Now, stop with the story about Godzilla attacking Wal-Mart during a hurricane and swallow your pride. Fit your script to your locations, and most especially, to your budget.

WRITER'S BLOCK? WATCH MOVIES YOU HATE

Go back to earlier in the process. You have a location. You understand story. You even have an idea. Only, now you've encountered writer's block. What's this? It means your fingers just won't move on your cousin's fifty-year-old Russian-made keyboard.

What should you do?

You've probably been watching movies you absolutely love. But have you been watching them and really reverse engineering how the stories are told? Have you looked at the scripts for some of your favorite films? They're probably online for free!

Keep in mind that you're creating a short film, not a feature-length epic starring Patrick Stewart as the King of England. Have you considered what a script for a short film version of *Raiders of the Lost Ark* would look like for a low-budget production? Probably one or two sets indoors and outdoors, maybe a classroom setting, maybe a dig site, some small artifacts (made yourself out of sculptor clay and paint), cool costumes, a lot of dialogue to carry the film. Minimal action. Some cheap stunts. Voila!

Also watch a movie in the genre you really like and analyze your feelings afterwards. What makes you love that film? It might really help get those fingers rolling on the keypad.

Rickey loves *Terminator 2* because he can relate to John Connor. (We think Rickey wants to save the world or something. Who knows? Rickey could actually *be* John Connor.) He also loves *Jurassic Park* because as a kid he wanted to see real dinosaurs. Just loves them. Imagine how that love of film gets his fingers flicking the keys.

Nicholas loves *Dead Poets Society*. He says the film makes him feel sad and passionate about literature all at once. (The guy just has no trouble writing about sad-sack literary types.) He also loves *Lost In Translation* because it feels otherworldly in its own way. You can literally examine your feelings after dozens of viewings of your favorites. Do it!

How do you feel after seeing *Sin City, Do the Right Thing, The Conjuring, Star Wars Episode I* (lamesauce), or *Star Wars: The Empire Strikes Back* (yay!)? All right, all right, make sure you examine films you *love* for this exercise.

Now watch something you *hate* in a genre specifically related to your film.

The reason behind watching a movie you think is terrible will help prevent all that bad stuff from trickling into your script. We dislike predictable movies that try to seem unpredictable but aren't. They leave a mess of the storyline (remember *story*? We know you do). We want to write a good twist at the end with enough story to keep people interested long enough to see the twist. Surprise your audience. Lead them like fish into a net, monkeys into a barrel. Whatever. Just lead them. Then smack them square in the face with that twist! Okay, you're inspired. No more writer's block. Go! Go! Go!

WELL-BEHAVED FILMS RARELY MAKE HISTORY

You might not be a songwriter or rapper, but if you want people to watch your film, you better figure out your gimmick as if you're the biggest rock star in the world.

In songs, the *hook* might be the main chorus or certain beats, or if hip-hop, a repeating phrase. This motif of words or beats is what pulls you in. You love a song? You're probably humming that motif, which in other words is that piece's creative gimmick.

In film, just like in music, we don't want gimmicks to be stupid or dull. We do want to raise some eyebrows with themes or types of characters that constantly grab your attention. Laurel Thatcher Ulrich once wrote that "well-behaved women seldom make history." Well-behaved films rarely make history, either.

When we made *Naked Zombie Girl*, the name alone was gimmick enough to grab attention. Our gimmick was obviously the idea that both sex and zombies sell (but not sex with zombies—gross!). While there's no sex or nudity in the movie, the sexual element in the title alone still drives people to watch the short film. A more common example is *Fast and Furious*. It's not brain surgery to consider their gimmick: cars. How about *Blade Runner*? Androids. *Star Wars*: duh. You get the idea. Gimmicks can be huge motifs, or themes, or they can be a certain character type, hero, or outlandish blend of genres. This is where your creativity comes in. You're the superstar filmmaker. Experiment!

"GOTCHA" TIMING IN SCRIPTS

While writing your award-winning short film, keep visual-timing in mind. Often what you think reads well in a script doesn't always translate into good visual elements. For instance, jokes in films have to be visual in nature. They also need comedic timing. Let's say your script has a joke about a limping guy named Jim. Some other characters are poking fun about the guy. Just how funny will the joke be if your audience never sees Jim limping down the street in a naked-day parade, or into a herd of Chihuahuas, or changing his limp from left to right depending on the weather?

Now, don't go thinking we bully people with limps! We're known for having some pretty tasteless gags. Jokes can be about anything. The point is to use visuals and include that all-important comedic timing. If Jim enters the scene before there's a set-up for a joke, the viewer might not have a reaction other than, "Why is that person walking with a limp?" Most of all, you'll never write funny scenes if you don't try. Give it some effort.

You're getting to know all those little twists in your scenes from the story you scrawled on your bedroom wall, but screenwriting really captures the visual elements of story and surprise. Get descriptive! In the horror genre, the visual is often a buildup of various intense or scary images. You need to be able to visualize not only the terrifying aspects of your locations, but how locations, characters, and props can visually tie-in with horror twists—those *gotcha* or pop-out moments. Just consider the idea that instead of showing the monster, your camera reveals part of a creature for the tiniest of seconds. Put that in the script! Be creative with your reveals! Let your audience's imagination scare them, too!

Since you're the director, be extra creative with your descriptions. For instance, in horror, long hallways with the lights off can really be that much scarier. Make notes. Your screenwriting program probably has an area for *action* or *director* notes. Your notes are important for your script and are your reference. That way, when you're shooting, you don't forget the point of the shot (let's just say there's a reason Rickey and his old buddy Jason named the production company Hectic Films). Note: this is not how you would submit a script to a contest or agent. You're filming this masterpiece yourself. And since you're on a budget, and you're the next Tarantino, and you're the writer-director, lead actor, cinematographer, sound editor...pretty much everything, then you need all the help you can get.

So, add lots of notes, and most of all, be creative!

More dialogue tricks

Uh oh. You can't think of any dialogue that seems right for two of your characters. First, if you haven't already, spend some time on their backstory. Who are they? What do they like? Now get back to your scene and consider their environment. Make them talk about something in the room while discussing whatever it is they're arguing about. Maybe one of your characters loves peanut butter. Maybe he or she mentions needing some for a sandwich. How about the opening scene of *Reservoir Dogs*? Ever studied that? There's a discussion about pop culture mixed with a dangerous *job*. Through simple dialogue you get to know each character. Try something similar.

The production bible

The Production Bible is an important set of documents you create that includes all your notes about your film. While you can create a digital copy, a hard copy is most important. Organize it. Include all elements of your film: script, project overview, design, schedules. Add everything that isn't in your script but is a part of your story— backstories, motivations, descriptions of settings. Everything. Trust us. This will make your characters noticeably solid on screen.

Incorporating the "big scene"

In case you've forgotten, many feature-length movies and short films have at least one big scene that makes you go, "Wow! How'd they do that?" If you haven't already, consider one big scene idea. Maybe it's a special effect for your ten minute sea adventure, or a crazy head-bursting, spine-ripping death for your slasher horror film. You never know, this could be the scene you had in mind when you started writing this script. How do you think *Alien* was created in the first place? Stomach spawn pop-out! Yes! First of its kind! Anyway, don't forget to consider, "How much can I get away with here?" Why? Have you thought about your location? Are you planning on getting fake blood *everywhere*? You want to make sure the owners of your location are cool with it. They are? *Yessss*. Time for more planning!

Chapter Four

WHAT TO DO WITH YOUR $2,000?

Planning and Budget Made Easy

S till think you're ready to start filming? You've got your big script and a temporary title for it, *Factory of Souls*. You even have a number of stealth locations. Feeling pretty good about yourself, aren't you? We can see you oozing with confidence, chomping at the bit to start production.

Hate to say it—you forgot some things.

Haven't bought a camera yet? What are you going to do, film with your thumb out in front of your face? It's not going to record or be in HD. Where are your actors? Your script calls for three cop characters. Several scenes have zombie extras. Where's your crew? Lighting? Sound? Costumes? Ahh! The horror!

But wait. You can't buy a camera. You can't recruit actors. You can't do anything. Stomach churning? You're a mess all over again. Want to know why? Because you haven't planned a thing! Trust us, you need to get organized, especially with your money. Detailed even. You only have $2,000, remember? And you already owe for locations. We hope you didn't screw that up. You didn't just spend $500 renting an old barn with horse bones in it, did you? Wait a minute, you do have $2,000, don't you?

Now, don't worry. Well, okay. Filmmakers *worry*. It's what we do. We have anxiety, and usually we're control freaks. We have to be. Why? Because we have plans and we need to stick with them. Oh ho! Finally admitting you didn't make any kind of plan? Now you're also admitting you don't have $2,000, let alone the eight dollars for that fancy coffee you got for free because your best friend works at a drive-thru? (Extra points!) That's the only way to get that overpriced crap!)

All right, aspiring filmmaker, it's time to show you how to raise funds and how to budget. For starters, you need to know how to fundraise without robbing convenience stores using that fake prop gun and ski mask you already blew some cash on. It might get you some free candy bars along with that jail time, but it won't fund your film.

All right, time to take this handy book, sit in a quiet place, and make some notes. You've got some serious planning to do. Go ahead, scrawl in the margins if you have to. It's okay. It's your book. You did pay for it, didn't you?

PLAN A: CROWDFUNDING

Ready to raise money? Got your cardboard sign so you can start begging like that homeless guy down the street you always see carrying a tall can? You gave your last dollar to that guy? Nice job. He's *good*. Maybe you should recruit him to help raise funds.

Now that we know you're desperate for cash to make your flick, we're going to put the cart before the horse. The thing is, you don't normally crowdfund unless you have an idea how much money you need. That usually means you have to figure out your entire budget beforehand. But since you've never done this before, we're going to reverse engineer the whole shebang.

Set the budget for this project at $2,000 big ones!

Like we said, you're supposed to budget first to figure out what you really need. Who knows? You may only need $100 bucks to shoot your film (Yeah, right.)

Now go ahead and do some research. Choose a crowdfunding site from any number of them, like IndieGoGo, Kickstarter, or GoFundMe. Read the fine print, set up your profile, all the good stuff. Think twice about Kickstarter. Didn't reach your goal? It won't allow you to keep donations unless you do. Bye bye.

Ready to set that monetary goal? Hold on one more second. With crowdfunding you have to pay a fee. The fee is paid through a percentage of campaign donations. That means you must incorporate fees into your goal. And there's more. You need money for *prizes* or *perks*, as well as shipping. All those t-shirts you're promising donors that say *Factory of Souls*? Someone has to pay for them. For example: you need $2,000 for your film. Your campaign goal might need to be set at $2,200 (depending on fee charges and all those perks). You also need to think of any type of advertising budget. Posters, stickers, a tape-gun so you can plaster your posters everywhere, and a button maker so you can hand pins out like candy to your donors... Like we said, we want to help you roll in the cheddar. But you might need to set that budget at $2,400. Up to you.

Now's the time for a plan of attack filled with press releases, artwork, and videos.

You are a filmmaker, aren't you? Does your film company have a logo? How about one for your film? Hey, catch up, already! Get your artwork in order. You need it for your crowdfunding video, not to mention on all those t-shirts and hats.

About that *video*. Every crowdfunding campaign needs one. Make it very short, only one or two minutes in length. Make sure the lighting and sound are solid. Even if you're shooting with your phone, you still need to take proper filmmaking techniques into consideration. People who don't know you will not invest in you. They'll think your movie is going to be a turd if your video looks awful.

Don't forget to be yourself, be honest, and don't be a douchebag. Oh, and look at the camera and act confident even if you're terrified!

Here are our basic three topics to cover in your crowdfunding video:

1. *Who*: describe you and your dream.
2. *What*: show story and art concepts.
3. *How & Why*: how you will use donations/why you need money so bad.

Next, you need to think of your *perks* for your campaign (hint: if you consider them beforehand, you might be able to show one off in your video). A perk is something that the people donating will receive as a thank you. For example, donate thirty bucks and we'll send you a poster in the mail. Donate $1,000 and we'll send you an autographed zombie head cast from the mold used in our film. *Yassss!* Now let's break down the cost of the perk. Let's say shipping costs us five bucks with the price of the poster. That's five bucks off of your donation proceeds; factor in those costs. A good one that works for us is five bucks gets your name in the credits of the film. Digital giveaways are much easier than creating and sending zombie heads and posters, though you might want all three. Please? (Insert zombie monster sounds.)

What about *press releases*? Did you really just interrupt us with that? If you don't know what a press release is, you'll learn soon enough. Our suggestion? *Google*. Seriously, you can download press release templates off the Internet and just fill in the blanks. Do some research about what goes in them: the who, what, when, where and why about your project (mostly stuff from your crowdsourcing promotional video). Read a lot of samples before you write your own. While you're at it, read a lot of crowdfunding pages, too. Got it? Okay. Keep in mind the outside world has no idea who you are. Not yet, anyway. Boy, will they find out! In the meantime, you have to be descriptive about how you're going to pull this dang movie off. So download the press release template and slap that thing together. Make sure your contact info is correct and choose a date to launch your project.

Now you have a video and a press release! Cha-ching! These are the seeds that sprout money! (Said some wise men: us!)

Have you uploaded your press release info and video to your crowdfunding site? Do that. Don't forget to add your perk list.

One more thing: before you launch your campaign, talk to some trusted friends and family. Get them on board with what you're doing about raising funds. They'll want those perks! That way they'll donate as soon as your project goes *live*.

FACEBOOK AND GETTING ON THE NEWS

Have you started a Facebook page for your film? Get on it. Invite everyone on your personal Facebook page to join. Then create an event for your crowdsourcing campaign and set the date of the event for the last day of your campaign (yes, crowdfunding requires start and end dates). Make sure you post once in a while within the Facebook event. This will remind your Facebook audience that you have something going on.

Press releases are like fish. If you toss a fish on the ground it won't do anything but flop around. Next thing you know, someone is slapping you for being mean to a slimy old catfish. Put a fish in water and guess what? It *swims*. This means your press release needs to be swimming! Start emailing and/or faxing it to your local newspaper and radio and TV stations. Someone might want to do a story on your fundraising. Why not? You're cool. Your movie is cool, too! You might get an interview where you can talk about your film! Your film genre is horror? Try sending your press release to horror blogs and horror magazine websites. Make sure they don't frown on this. Some sites want to seek out their own info. Check their *news submission* pages. You can also search for free websites that let you upload your press release. Some might make you pay a few bucks. No matter how you do it, just get your press release out there.

TRANSPARENCY

COLOUR SERVICE

Email lists: these are a powerful tool. Try and get as many email addresses as you can from people you know and those who might be interested in donating to your project. This is the most powerful way to get people involved in your project. Why not aim for one hundred emails to start off? You gotta start somewhere. Then go to MailChimp or Tiny Letter and set up a free newsletter campaign. That's right. It's *free*. Well, it will cost you some sleep. But we don't care about that. You're a filmmaker. You'll sleep when you're dead. Now, send out those newsletters once every week or two. No more than that. Don't forget to include links to your crowdfunding campaign. Hooray!

PLAN B: MONEY THE "OLD-FASHIONED WAY"

Be creative with your crowd funding promotions

Sell candy bars, just not your soul. Didn't you know? You sold most of your soul already just deciding to be a filmmaker. Good luck getting your old life back. You're too far in now. By the way, we know you're still barely making rent and need some more cash for that film. Have you considered a car wash? Pull out the old lawn mower. You know what to do. Knock on those doors. Are you desperate enough to get a credit card? Most limits are right around $2,000, right? We only recommend that route to the most desperate of filmmakers. Debt is a sorrowful thing. You can also ask local businesses if they might like to sponsor your film. Make sure to offer putting their name on it as one of the producers. You'd be surprised how many business owners jump at the chance to do some different types of advertising.

One final act of desperation: stand on the side of the road and ask for money. Think we're kidding? Rickey once stood on a street corner with George the Giant from the movie *Big Fish* for two days just trying to get people to donate to the Western short film, *Mable*. True story. Look it up.

THE BUDGET

Like we said, normally you figure out this part first. Well, right after you have a script. But *you* do things the cheap way, don't you? (We taught you well.) You found your location(s). Awesome! You wrote a script around those locations, keeping in mind you didn't want to spend a lot of money. The fewer everything, as you now know, the cheaper the film is to make. Now follow carefully: make some notes and be creative. Why? Because although we're going to tell you how to spend those two nickels, they're still *your* nickels. Besides, you're smart. You might discover a few budget tricks of your own. Got that pen? All right, let's go...

CRAFTY FOOD SERVICES ON YOUR SHOOT: $200

Let's get basic here. People need to eat. Feeding everyone on your film set is priority number one. Isn't there a saying? *Happy wife, happy life?* Not bad. We like that. How about we come up with something similar for your team? *Happy crew and actors, better movie.* After all, that's what we're in this for—a better movie than if you would have made it without this book.

In the movie biz there's an appointed person in charge of feeding the staff. They call this glorified caterer *craft services*. On the big sets they even have chefs. Yeah. That's a little out of your budget unless Grandma has volunteered to make her famous okra and pig's feet stew for your crew. Before you say yes to her, ask yourself—do I really want Granny on the set? *Cough.*

Anyway, provide healthy snacks and drinks (and unhealthy ones too if you really want to be real about it). That way, your crew can grab something to eat or drink throughout each shooting day. We suggest that for your two-to-three-day shoot to budget yourself for at least *ten bucks a person* for food costs.

MGB BEHIND THE SCENES

You can also hit up restaurants and see if they will cater for credit in your movie. It works. See how thrifty you can be! While on a film shoot, our man Terry McGhee actually scored free pizzas two nights in a row! Free has zero cost when it comes to food, people! They got their credit in the film, and we were happy to give it.

Make sure there's *no booze*. Trust us. You don't want drunks screwing up your shoot.

One more food trick: consider the sneaky potluck. A great way to not only get free food, potlucks allow your staff and actors to show off their mama's hot jambalaya!

Hey, you've got a movie to shoot. Gotta think fast!

THE CAMERA: $0-$500

We're working with the idea that you don't have a camera. Already do? You're ahead of the game. You'll have funds to allocate somewhere else. For those who don't, we recommend using a DSLR (Digital Single-Lens Reflex). In 2008, the arrival of the Canon Mk II changed the game for indie filmmakers by allowing everyone to shoot HD video off non-video-only camera. These cameras function really well in low light, you can interchange lenses, and they're unassuming if you need to be stealthy. Think about it. You can look like you're taking a still when really you're making a movie. Sneak attack!

Of course, you can shoot on anything you want. As long as you use great lighting techniques, you should be fine! You can get a Canon DSLR at Costco for around $500. You can always hire someone for two days, too, but why not acquire your own equipment? Besides, you're really limiting yourself on pick-up shots if you have to hire someone. Of course, there's the $200 version of hiring someone. A lot of up and coming DPs (Director of Photography, aka, the guy working the camera) will have his own equipment. That might be an option. He or she might even do it for free.

dlsr camera

LIGHTING: $100

Our recommendation for lighting rigs is director Robert Rodriguez's way, but updated. In *El Mariachi*, he used a shop light. A more common name is bell lights. Sometimes the light temperature on these gets a little warm (more on this later). So we do something a little different. *Square lights* are battery-operated dimmable lights you can get off Amazon for about thirty dollars. We shot *Naked Zombie Girl* using only two of them. You should get three. If you want to upscale, consider spending $200 on a lighting kit from Cowboy Studio. Cowboy Studio is one of the most affordable light brands.

The "bell light" and the "square light"

ACTING TALENT: $$$?

You can do just about anything here. Maybe you have friends who can act. Maybe you want to do a casting call. Maybe you want to spend more money on the production, so you just want free talent. Who can't act, right? That's why you're a great director. You can discover talent! Remember this: a lot of actors just want to be seen on screen. That's all they want. Most don't want this as a career and probably have day jobs or parents to care for them. So think about this: *you're actually paying them by putting them in your movie.* Hey, you don't have a lot of money, right? Well, just don't be a jerk about it. You're not doing anyone favors if you think everyone has to work for you for free. It's just that right now you're on a tight budget, and you need help. Lots of communities don't even have filmmakers. People get really excited about movies. They band together, help out. You'd be surprised how much talent gets donated. On your next movie, pull some of them in and try to pay them something. Note: if an actor has to travel over thirty minutes to get to your set, you need to at least pay them some gas money. With actors, it's always a "hurry up and wait," so keep them happy on the set. Don't be a prima donna dirtbag. Treat everyone with respect. It will keep them from walking off your project.

LOCATIONS: $100

We've talked about this. Still, it's good to have a little cushion. For example, your short film takes place at a seedy motel. Well—you can use thirty bucks to rent the room, and then ten bucks for disinfectant. You may also need to "grease the wheels" on a location owner. You know. Give him or her a little extra. Either way, keep $100 aside for locations.

THE CREW: $200

You need to take care of your crew. These guys and gals are the heart of your project. They might be shooting the film, helping with the food, building sets, you name it. It might only be three of you on the crew, but those other two are invaluable. Don't expect your crew to work for free. Make sure to discuss pay with them before you shoot.

SOUND: $300

Can't afford a sound guy? There's a little sound device called a *Zoom H1*. You can get these off the web for about a hundred bucks. If you can go a little bigger, get the *H4N*. You also need a microphone to go with it. We recommend Rode Microphones' cheapest model: around $150. Now you just need an SD card. Get something name-brand. Only use this card for your audio.

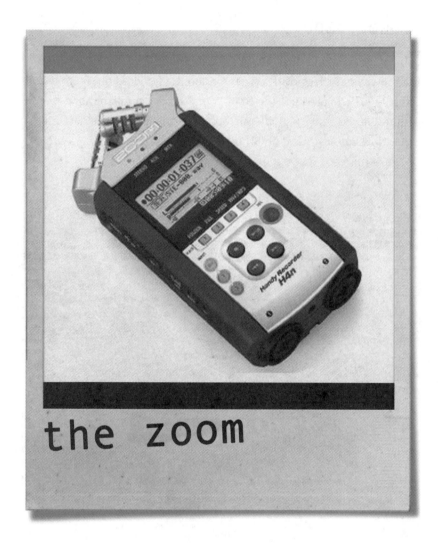

the zoom

MAKEUP: $100

Depending on what your script calls for, this number could go up
or down. A hundred bucks is a good placeholder. This could also be
your special effects budget. Don't forget Karo syrup for blood and
firecracker explosions!

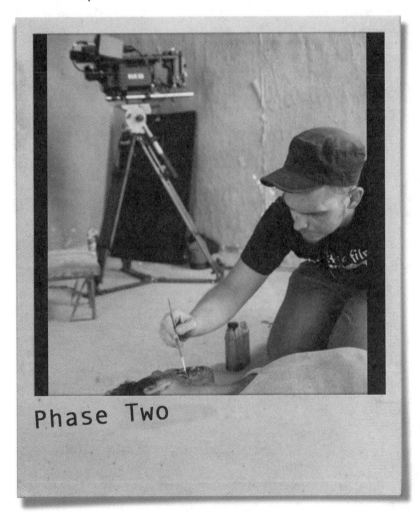

Phase Two

HARD DRIVE: $100

You can get a hard drive for around a hundred bucks. YOU MUST GET A HARD DRIVE. Don't go cheap on us now. It's important that you keep your film in its "reel" so that you can keep all your video, audio, and pictures on this device. Always try to keep a backup, even if it's stored on your grandmother's computer. Trust us, you don't wanna lose this shit.

get a Hard drive
any brand will work

CAMERA SLIDER: $100

Camera sliders give you more panning and angle options and mount to a tripod. You can go two ways with this. If you don't have the money in your budget, then you can watch a DIY tutorial on YouTube on how to make one. We suggest if you want the smoothness of a moving shot, then spend the hundred bucks. Maybe you know someone with a slider and can save this money altogether.

any dslr slider
will do

POST-PRODUCTION: $100

We recommend using Adobe Creative Cloud. Adobe's software gives users access to a suite of programs, including the editing program, Premiere Pro, which Rickey swears by. Depending on how fast you edit, you will be able to cut your short film for ten to twenty dollars. If you already have an editing program that you trust, then use it. We'll give you some basic editing tips later in the book.

MUSIC AND SOUND: $50

For a fee, you can utilize sound effects and music on AudioJungle.com. *Do not use* copyrighted music, or anything for that matter, that you do not have the right to use. Something as simple as a song could kill your project, or get your film kicked out of a festival. By the way, have you thought about hitting up local bands and singer-songwriters in your area? There are lots of people online, too. You never know who will let you use their music in your film if you don't start asking.

DVDS, POSTERS, AND PROMOTIONS: $200

Your cousin who says he knows how to design posters just offered to make one for free. All he can do are stick drawings. Sure you want to use him? We recommend finding someone with graphic art skills. You can find skilled designers on sites like Guru.com. They might cost you, but so what? Your poster needs to be great. It needs to lure people into donating to your crowdfund, and make them want to see your film when you have a screening. Better yet, have a few poster designs made. Release them in stages.

Many times filmmakers don't think about how important poster drawings are and how they come into play. Think *life or death*. Can we be any clearer? You also need a little cash to promote your film online. Boost posts for a dollar a day on Facebook and Twitter with the leftovers. See how easy that is? You're getting it! Budget it! You also need to make sure you save some money for printing posters. Add flyers, too, while you're at it. They're one of the best ways to get your film noticed when you're at a film festival or when you're on the streets. Make them look really catchy and professional (again, don't use your cousin's stick drawings). Almost forgot, you'll need DVDs for screening your project! No need to get fancy. You can do them yourself. So, just budget the cost of a package of DVDs.

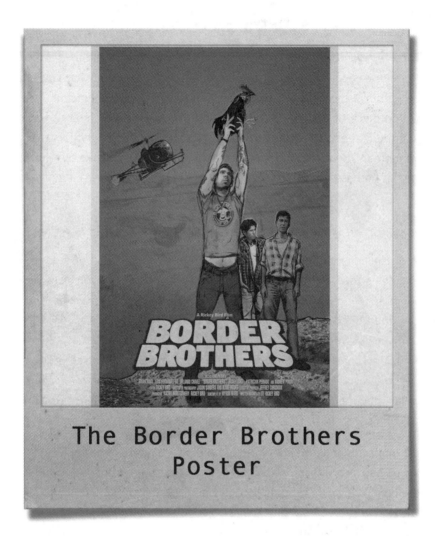

The Border Brothers
Poster

Boost your posts!

Reminder: If you want people to take you seriously, take yourself seriously. Being prepared as a filmmaker makes all the difference. So take care of all your promotional costs while planning.

FESTIVAL ENTRIES: $100

The average film festival costs twenty to fifty dollars. They increase fees the closer it gets to submission deadlines. Think about this, too: your chances of getting your short film into a festival on a last-minute entry could turn up nothing. So think way ahead. Here's another idea: pick three film festivals where you're willing to pay submission fees. Then for the rest of your fests, search online for free festivals for other possible entries. By the way, have you checked out FilmFreeway.com? It's really one of the best ways to connect with film festivals.

-ScreamFest -
The Chinese Theater Hollywood

WEBSITE AND HOSTING: $50

Finally, your film not only needs its own Facebook and Twitter, it needs a website. We recommend using GoDaddy.com and registering a domain for your film. If you have no website-building skills, you can sign up for a site builder on GoDaddy. They break down the process so even the worst web novice can put together a site. Pump your new page full of whatever you have: artwork, press release, trailers, videos. Take selfies on set with your smartphone, or get someone on set to do it. Post all over your site and social media. Give people a reason to keep checking up on your website! Oh yeah, most of all, budget for your site or it won't happen.

make a good website

Chapter Five

THIS MOVIE NEEDS STYLE!

Set and Costume Themes

Oh no. Frustrated again? Sitting by yourself in that coffeehouse staring at your notebook like you're the most lost of lost souls? We've been there, twiddling our thumbs, plotting diagrams to take over the world. It seems easier than making a short film!

We understand. This film is your baby. First question: Did you change its diaper?

Just kidding.

It's overwhelming finding the right *look* for your film. Film styles are recognizable film techniques that give value to your work. You have a lot to think about. Style includes frame rate, coloring, shooting style, sound, mise-en-scène, dialogue, cinematography, attitude, costumes, sets... That's a lot to cover. Too much! This is your first short film, so let's break some of it down in language you and I understand.

You might choose to shoot your short film using that popular shaky-camera-found-footage style, á la the *Blair Witch Project.* Not to mention those backwoodsy sets and costumes to go with it: an abandoned house, trees. Don't forget trees. Didn't we say this already? Add some outdoorsy costumes. You know that whole worn Patagonia thrift store look? (Don't tell your friends we said that.) Include some cool witchy trinkets, not the Harry Potter whimsical kind. Oh, and a witch costume, something dark, terrifying, incredibly disturbing, and BLACK. Start your research! Find a seamstress. Create! Experiment! (But keep those costs down.) And practice those shooting techniques.

Maybe you like the look of our horror short, *Naked Zombie Girl*, and its grindhouse style—the seventies, grainy, dark, weird, lots of undead zombies, a beat-up car, and the open road. Make the world your set! You can always go Old West like our Western short, *Mable*: lots of Civil War-era costumes, cowboy hats, women in poufy lace, a horse, a saloon (that we literally stumbled on through some crazy connections), and lots of rustic set pieces, mostly filmed in bright daylight in the great outdoors. You got it! Do a variation. Vaqueros in drag! We'll cheer you on!

Could be you're more into *Sin City*. You like that comic book feel to your sets. Lots of suits and classy dresses for the costumes. Add alleys and buildings, stark contrasts with shadows and light, and experimental stylized filters that make any low-budget set look cool. You can do it! Research!

Could be you want a series of epic nature shots and sets like those in *The Revenant*. Good luck freezing your you-know-what off. Go climb a mountain, as they say, and start researching different types of encampments. Do it!

Could be you need to stay with what you know. Okay! A film you love is *Snakes on a Plane*. We knew it! That one's a love-hate relationship with us. All those cramped quarters. Those close-ups. The rubber snakes. The working class feel and dark lighting. You can re-create that atmosphere! And the costumes are half-dressy to dressy. You got that! It doesn't matter if your story isn't set on a plane. Just try to emulate the style!

Are you the kind of filmmaker who likes lots of suits, drab lighting, and guns (not to mention, guys filling their cheeks with cotton balls who sound like they have asthma)? You should probably consider *The Godfather* or *Donnie Brasco* as a style reference. You can't go wrong with a gangster dinner scene. Set that table to fit your characters: fancy dining or home cooked meal. Rickey loves the movie *Planet Terror* by Robert Rodriguez. It's a grindhouse zombie film that inspired *Naked Zombie Girl*. Just like Rose McGowan in *Planet Terror*, our heroine, Barbara, is an ass-kicking lady in the middle of the zombie apocalypse. Oh, how those old drive-in horror movies tormented so many parents in the Seventies! Not us! One thousand heart emojis, please! Make those sets greasy and dirty and the film shaky and grainy.

All this talk about style is still making you a little crazy, huh?

The obvious answer is to take things slow.

(You don't always have to by hyper ninjas like us!)

Think everything through and you'll be okay as you pick your style. This is your *visual* voice, so choose wisely and roll with it.

It's okay to blend styles, too. You might already have an idea. Your action-comedy has lots of stunts, right? Have you checked your notes? You probably figured some of this out as you were writing your script. Did you scribble anything that said, Bruce Lee? How about Chuck Norris, Donnie Yen, or Jackie Chan? If you did, you were probably making a stylistic reference. There you go! See? Easier than you thought.

Running around Bakersfield getting shots for The Lackey

Maybe your locations are alleyways and old brick buildings. Sounds like you might consider some kind of "Asia meets New York" stylistic theme with lots of gangster costumes, New York cop uniforms, dark brick alleys, and graffiti. Maybe a little like the 1996 film *Rumble in the Bronx*. Ever see it? Jackie Chan is a Hong Kong policeman in New York. They actually filmed in Vancouver. You can see mountains in some scenes. Very *not* New York. But who cares, right? Suspension of disbelief. What mattered were the fight scenes, the lighting, the costumes, and the way the film was purposely over-dubbed to make the movie seem retro and cool, like it was stylistically blending Asian gangster films and American gangster films all in one. The crew actually had to paint graffiti every day of the shoot and take it down in the evenings. Lots of work gave it that certain look!

We shot our film *The Lackey* on the streets of downtown Bakersfield, California. If you've ever been to Bakersfield, you know its downtown doesn't have much to it. *The Lackey* feels like it was shot in a huge city! People actually came up to us thinking we shot the film in New York.

Yeah, um, sure we did.

Fooled you, suckas!

The point is, you might desire a gritty New York gangster style even if you live in California or Wisconsin. As long as you're creative, you got it!

DON'T MAKE STUPID COSTUME CHOICES

Check this one out. Let's say you picked a *Men in Black* style movie. You want the guys and girls in suits. You even kept in mind that *suits cost money*. So you realize you have an old suit in the closet. Then again, the suit is green *and* plaid. Did you really want to rename your film, *Girls in Black and that One Boy in Green Plaid*? Look, if you can't do something right with wardrobe, don't do it.

When Rickey guest-starred in an indie Western, most everyone appeared on set in authentic Wild West costumes. Then BOOM! A guy shows up wearing a bright white t-shirt! ROOKIE MOVE!

We perform the sign of the cross every time we're reminded of this blunder.

What? You don't get it? Do you really want your audience wondering if form-fitting Hanes tees were around in the Old West?

Misplaced wardrobe in your film means you're visually highlighting *mistakes*. Don't get us wrong. You have to cut corners. There will be *faux pas*.

Just don't purposely hurt your project.

You need to make some tough decisions with wardrobe. You're starting to get that. But maybe it hasn't completely sunk in. Here's another example. The producers for our film *Phase Two* weren't the brightest on set. They didn't take our advice about wardrobe. Why? The characters in the film were in the desert. One of the actors thought his wardrobe would be awesome if he wore a tank top. Uh oh. The producers agreed. *No-o-o!* Two things happened here. Through the course of the film the actor's arms tanned. Some scenes didn't match because of his changing skin tone! This also sucked for the sunburned actor, proving the basic point we all know, that you can't run around in the desert with a tank top and no sun protection! The producers and the actor quickly regretted their bumble-headed decision.

on the set of MABLE

Temperature for style!

Along with your look, here's something else to consider: *temperature.* No, things are not heating up in here. What we're referring to is *light temperature.* What kind of tone do you want in your film? Cool colors or warm tones? You don't want your shots to be a different color for different angles in the same scene.

Did you get that? Pay attention where you set up your lights. Your scenes need to be lit with the same brightness and same temperature in each shot. You can control some of this in post-production, but trust us, you don't want to rely on fixing all your scenes after principal photography has been completed. Also, you can slightly change the color if you need to between scenes to set the mood of the moment. Enough of that—we'll give you more lighting tips in an upcoming chapter...

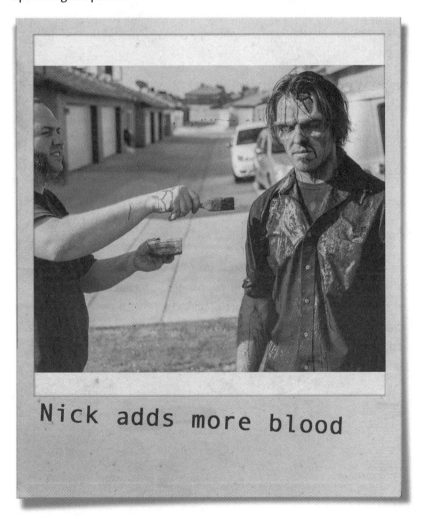

Nick adds more blood

Stock up on kill clothes

So this guy in your movie is wearing Grandpa's tweed jacket as part of his wardrobe. His character also happens get brutally slain in an epic SFX scene, complete with fake blood, tears, and even burn marks in the clothing. You didn't think about having more than one jacket available for your actor, did you? Uh oh. During your epic human destruction scene, fake blood flies and part of the jacket is purposely torn and burnt. Then, while the cameras are still rolling, some *schlep* walks through the background eating a Subway sandwich. "What?" he says.

"What?" you scream. "You not only ruined our only take—that was our only Grandpa jacket!"

Not to mention—your ham sandwich.

What a dick.

Film ruined. Find a new career.

Now wait. Take a deep breath.

You can prevent this kind of screw up with what we like to call *kill clothes*. If you have characters in your short film that are scripted to get splattered, provide the actors playing them with two, if not three, sets of the same wardrobe. Remember: lighter colors on your murder victim makes the blood stand out better! Oh, and you might *not* want death scenes in suits. Once again, those are expensive!

Chapter Six

HEY, YOU LOOK LIKE A STAR!

How to Get the Best Acting Talent for Less

Time for that casting call!

In case you didn't know—your film could be a hot potato because of *who* you put in it. Hey, even if your short film only calls for *you* and one other actor (because you want to be a star, too!), you still need to know how to kidnap, we mean, *cheaply acquire*, acting talent to help maximize your film's production value.

So let's get started...

The late great
Jim Padgett in
The Badge 2

Acting talent can help your film have the look and feel of being much bigger than a $2,000 movie. Never fear. When you're like us—*broke as heck*—you'll still find a way to get those B-movie names to give your script the time of day.

Like we said, we have solutions.

Now, some actors won't be as willing as others to be on camera for free or on a film with a tight budget. But that's okay, because we have candy in our van. Muahahaha! All right, enough with the dumb jokes…

CASTING CALL

Film casting is the selection process you go through when picking actors or actresses for roles in your movie. Once you have your script, casting is simple.

First, print up some copies of your masterpiece…

Stop! You're on a budget, remember? Don't print a hundred copies of your script! Whew, that was close. You need to turn a couple script pages into what we call *sides*. You can print these short pieces on quarter sheets of paper. And you were going to waste all that money!

The next thing to do is blast social media with a clever flyer with all the information about your casting call (this is for all those non-B-movie-quality-actor roles). Include time, date, address, your film company name. All the good stuff. Don't forget a clear, simple heading, like, ACTING TALENT NEEDED FOR SHORT ACTION FILM. Include what you want your talent to look like: old, short, heavy set, thirtyish, skinny, and so on.

Sometimes you don't always get what you want. Let's say you're holding a casting call at a restaurant. Maybe you advertised in your flyer that your film needs a pudgy middle-aged blonde guy with a mullet. Sadly, the only middle-aged guy who showed up is bald. So what? Is he any good? Does he present a favorable reading? Does he seem believable? Just go with it. Don't delay your movie because of details you can't control. If you really need him to be blonde, give him a wig! Better yet—embrace baldness. Hooray!

Rickey filming with Aaron

CASTING PERFORMANCES

When casting, have actors give a couple of variations of performances with those *sides* you provided. Can they vary their emotions? Can they transition from happy to sad? How do they deal with tragedy? Can they freak out? Can they appear calm under pressure? Can they crumble to the ground like a broken-hearted child? During a casting call for *Border Brothers*, some of the actors read lines as if discovering a friend died.

Guess what? Those lines had nothing to do with the character's friend dying. We just needed to see the actors' *range*, which means how believable a performance might be if expressed through various emotions.

Tip: have someone from your crew read lines with the talent trying out for each part. That way you can watch an actor's reactions. The sign of a good actor is in the ability to react to another person. Watch for it. *Analyze.*

GETTING FRIENDS INTO THE "ACT"

So let's say only three people showed up to your casting call. Even though you made a sweet flyer and posted it all over social media, no one showed up. What do you do? Don't be discouraged. Hopefully you have a friend, someone you know willing to play a role in your film. When we shot our first short film, *Daft*, we asked co-workers to act in it. They showed up! Yes! Let's say your friends are willing, but don't fit your script. This is where you have to be creative. Make them fit into your story! This could be as simple as switching a couple of scenes around. Choose wisely, young *Padawan* apprentice.

THEATER ACTORS

Every town has some sort of theater scene. You know—where they perform plays and stuff? Go figure! Those actors and actresses might just want to appear in your short film! So how do you get their attention?

The first thing you need to do is to contact a theater. It's not hard. They probably have an email contact on their website. Tell them you're shooting a short film and you will only need actors for a couple of days. They'll probably be super excited! You can also go catch one of their plays. Why? Because you can watch the talent perform, see who might be a good fit for your project. Each of our films has at least one theater actor or actress. We enjoy the kind of presence they bring to filmmaking.

Who doesn't love Super Troopers!

THIS SIDE
TOWARD SCREEN

THE CELEBRITY FACTOR

What about those celebrity actors? What's so special about them? A couple of things: talent and name recognition (the celebrity factor).

Let's talk about celebrity factor for a moment. First, there are all types of celebrities. Local TV, theater, radio personalities, B-actors, not to mention the super famous.

What do they have in common? *Fandom*.

What's that? They have fans. Lots of 'em!

DJ Danny Spanks as Harrison Hamill in A Familiar Spirit

The recipe is simple: fans talk about *who* they're fans of. They support their favorite celebs. That means a celebrity's fans might support your short film!

When you're just starting out making short films, people are going to know the actors in your film more than they know you. The trick—of course—is to make a great film so you become a known entity. And you will! Just keep in mind that who you put in your film will gain you fans.

So who are these celebs?

In our short film, *A Familiar Spirit,* local DJ Danny Spanks makes an appearance. Does it matter that people probably don't recognize his name outside of our hometown? Not really. He has fans! Besides, he got us some attention for the project (and he was willing to appear in our film for free!). It was great! So whether an actor is a popular used-car salesman blasting crappy commercials, a DJ, or crazy TV weather girl, give them a shot! It might make something really awesome happen for your film.

What about B-movie actors? You know, the ones signing autographs at the horror conventions? They're really a great commodity and will take your film to new heights. If you can work with them, do it!

Hold on. Quit being so star struck! There *are* some things you need to find out when approaching them. Let's say you get in touch with a famous B-movie scream queen. You'd love for her to star in your little horror film, *The Night the Bugbear Ate My Sister.*

Is the actress able to work on non-union projects?

Uh oh. She can't?

If she belongs to the union, then politely say you'll get back in touch with her once you have enough money to do a union film. Who knows, maybe you can afford to pay union wages on your next short film.

Then again, maybe you're locked in to $2,000 film projects. Nothing wrong with that. Hectic Films prides itself on low-budget goodies.

The second question you need to ask: where does she live?

Why? Because she'll expect some compensation for travel expenses.

There could be wiggle room. Especially if you have some of your own gear. Remember, we budgeted you for a camera. You could use those allotted funds for travel money!

You might be able to figure out these questions by simply checking on IMDB (Internet Movie Database), Facebook, or an official fan page of the actor/actress of your choice. Yeah, we said it—you may have to Facebook stalk to figure out if you're about to shell out cash for an expensive plane ticket. The real question: is she worth it?

Theater acting bonus

Guess what? There are other bonuses when collaborating with your local theater. How about that it's a great place to hold casting calls? People see your casting call at a theater and it gives you a little more street cred. Second, theater actors usually know their lines pretty well. This is important in low-budget films. It means less takes when you have actors who can remember their lines! And let's not forget they may have local celebrity status that will get fans excited about your film! Bonus!

Brinke, George and DT on the set of MGB

Working with talent, from scream queen Brinke Stevens

Talent often takes up a large part of an indie shooting budget. The more an actor costs, the less money you'll have to spend elsewhere on the film. So, you'll have to figure out how much you can afford to pay. If you make the first offer, make it a fair one. If they make the first offer, then understand that the actor is usually informing you of their typical day-rate based on past hirings.

I like to support and mentor young filmmakers. Some gush about how much they enjoy my past movies and really want to work with me. Then, when I tell them my standard day-rate, I NEVER hear back from them again. Well, they could say, "We love you, but our budget can't afford that. How about $ xxx?" Or just say, "I'm sorry but I simply can't afford more than X." Too often, they drop the ball and drop out of sight. It's kind of insulting to me — they said they were such huge fans! And everybody loses. Please keep in mind that it's totally okay to negotiate with actors.

And always remember to treat your talent well. Offer them a written contract, and pay them before they leave the set. Utilize a shooting schedule and stick to it. No abusively long twenty-hour days. Have plenty of good food, and decent accommodations if they spend the night. Do not use real guns nor sharp knives! This sounds like common sense, but you'd be surprised.

Celeb Hack—Hectic Films 2-shot and the green screen

Oh boy. You can't get a B-movie celeb. And you can't afford travel expenses. What you gonna do? How about what we did in our film *The Lackey*? Try the ole Hectic Films 2-shot. This is where you film a scene in two locations but after editing it seems like one location. We use this method with multiple actors who need to appear at the same locale.

Vernon and Rickey at Action on Film Festival

In *The Lackey*, there's a scene where we had two thugs (actors, okay?) thrown into a limo with actor Vernon Wells (*Mad Max*).

Gotcha! Tricked you again! You're so easy to fool!

We used two different limos in the shot!

Director Shaun Piccinino shot one scene in the Los Angeles area with Vernon Wells. A few weeks later, we shot the thug portion in another limo in Bakersfield, California.

When we edited the two shots together, the scene became flawless.

It's easy to see the benefits: we added a celebrity to the film's line-up *and* saved a crap ton of travel money in the process. In addition, we came up with a few more scenes using the same B-star. We had Vernon Wells talk on the phone to more thugs. Then we inserted those scenes into the film. To the viewer, it seems like they're in the same city. We saved travel cash and an extra day of shooting.

There's also what we call the *Green Screen Drag-and-Drop*. This technique will allow you to shoot aspects of the same scene in two different locations by using a dummy stand-in (sorry to whoever is used as the dummy).

When you travel to the celeb, make sure to shoot him/her in front of a green screen. Then shoot a wall or background that is in the scene with the other actors. (Note: this works better if you know the lighting in the room so you can match it to your celeb.)

Shoot your celeb first, then follow up with your actors. That way you'll have a visual reference point in your film.

Example: your celeb is wearing a red shirt. In order to trick the audience you should do an over-the-shoulder shot (OTS) of a dummy actor wearing the same color shirt. After editing, it will look like the celeb is in the scene!

Where should I hold a casting call?

You can do a casting call anywhere you want. Preferably, have it at a public place. Not your home. Home is a weird choice. Besides, do you really want weirdos showing up to your mom's house? Haha. We couldn't resist... So what's a good place? Businesses might donate office space if you ask nicely. How about a restaurant with a private room? You can go low-scale pizza parlor with this. Just make sure there's privacy.

Chapter Seven

ACTION!
(ALMOST)

Shot Planning
and Storyboarding

"Is it time?" you ask. "I'm ready to make this movie!"

We're sure you are. But no—it's not time yet. You have some serious planning to do. So don't run out and start filming. That could be an expensive mess.

Reminder #127: you have limited resources.

You still have to organize your shots. You have to storyboard...

Quit pacing and worrying. It's not that bad. We've got lots of helpful ideas. So just keep reading this book, and start imagining your film taking on a life of its own. That's really what shot planning and storyboarding is all about: using your imagination constructively, so that each shot takes shape even before you start filming.

Storyboard from our pitch Devereux- Artwork by Craig Fraser

DIGITAL STORYBOARD

Now that you have all the pieces together, it's time to create digital storyboards of each scene you're going to be shooting.

What's a digital storyboard?

Almost forgot! Glad you asked. Storyboards are drawings, 3D renderings, or in this case, digital photos, that when laid out, resemble comic strip panels. These scene panels provide you and your crew with an overall sequential view of your short film. Anyone on the crew, whether you as the director, the cinematographer, or someone else, can examine your storyboards and tell what will visually happen in each scene.

For starters, print out your script, hold onto that notepad, and go to your location. Bring a smart phone or digital camera. If you already have a camera for shooting your film, then bring that. It's also important to bring someone to be a stand-in. Only your sister is available? Perfect. She's your model. Treat her well. You'll position her at film locations to give you a better understanding of actor placement in each shot.

Yes, we said *each* shot.

Suck it up and quit bellyaching. Your short film requires careful planning.

LOTS OF PLANNING.

While grabbing these storyboard shots, you need to mark scene numbers on pictures so you don't get confused. Trust us, these pics will pile up fast in a folder on your computer. So make notes. If you're using your phone, each photo you send to yourself has a corresponding number. Correspond those with each scene number in your notes. This will help you keep track. Use those numbers and a brief description of each scene shot. This will help you as you either upload your shots to some kind of free storyboarding program (once again, do your research!) or make panels on your own in Photoshop, Illustrator, or some other program. By the way, you can view all kinds of storyboards online as examples. Make Google your friend! How many times have we said this?

Storyboard from our pitch Devereux- Artwork by Craig Fraser

Walk through your location going through your script and grabbing the shots you want. Have your sister pose in the spirit of different characters. Hopefully she really gets into this! Carefully create the point of view (POV) you want in each shot as she takes the stance of the main focus in each scene. Use her to anchor your shots. Creatively consider every angle, every kind of trick camera shot you can do. Experiment with low angle, close-ups, medium shots, high angle... Make notes for when you want movement via dolly shots and more. We used GoPro cameras in our films for cut-scenes to crazy wide-angle POVs of claustrophobia. Maybe you can imagine some of those (look at our Shot Types list for more tips or create some of your own).

Use two or three people when you can if the scene calls for it. Be sure to transfer your photos into a folder on your newly acquired hard drive. Name the folder *Digital Storyboards* if you haven't already. It will save you some time, especially if you're able to go through the script in chronological order. Try and stay as close to chronological order as you can. It makes the pictures and videos easier to find when you go to make your panels, or if you're just keeping your photos to use as storyboards without description (our method).

If you have the camera you're going to use to film, this is a good time to get some *test footage*. Don't light anything, just grab a few different shots to see how the lighting naturally appears. Don't worry. Your sister doesn't have to be a good actress. But who knows—maybe she'll land a role!

Awesome! You're being organized right from the start! This is important, as you'll be sharing storyboards with your Director of Photography and crew.

Remember: *meticulous prep now makes for a better shoot later.*

We used this same method for our short film *As the Man Drives* to get an idea of what kind of lighting and shot selection we wanted. We shot the majority of the film in a vehicle as the two main actors shared dialogue. Beforehand, we went through all the shot possibilities we could for in-the-car-scenes, including those extra shots outside the car while it was moving.

You can't delay production, so plan, plan, plan. Time is money, and we don't know about you, but there isn't much money for us to be wasting. So prepare!

YOUR SHOT LIST

Time for one of those dreaded filmmaker's checklists...

You've grabbed all your storyboard shots. It's time to look over your notes and storyboards (or pictures) so you can start making your shot list. Think of this as a cheat sheet related to your storyboards and/or photo archive of shot selections.

By the way, your shot list includes every single shot in your movie.

Some folks get fancy with these. You don't have to.

Here are the basics...

List your shots in any order. We think the best method is to use the order of how you plan to shoot your short film. Maybe it makes sense to shoot the end of your film first based on limited access to locations. Maybe you need to shoot the middle acts first. Only you know the best arrangement. Do what saves you time and money! As long as you list scene numbers, you'll stay organized.

Mark locations on each section of the list. Let's say you only have two locations. Uncle Larry's place looks like a serial killer hangout. Grandma's humid apartment with the weird green kitchen is freaky, too. Instead of writing a paragraph on every line, just call Uncle Larry's place Location A. Grandma's apartment is Location B.

If you didn't get fancy with panels and you're only using photos, you'll still need those shot descriptions. Is it a wide shot? An extreme close-up? Be detailed, and don't forget to correspond with scene numbers.

Who knows, maybe you'll figure out your own method.

Whatever gets you through the madness and keeps you organized.

Establishing shots are really important!

Take time to get *establishing shots* for your film. If you're filming in a hospital room, you need to reinforce its authenticity by showing exterior. This makes the scene just a little more real for the viewer. Add movement to your establishing shot to make it feel more like a film and not a cheesy television commercial. This is where that camera slider you bought comes in handy. Grab a few different angles. If you have your camera, you can even grab these shots while gathering photos for storyboards.

Common shot types

Extreme Wide Shot (EWS). Establishing shot of a location.

Very Wide Shot (VWS). Show characters related to natural or man-made environments. Great for shots of cars exiting locations.

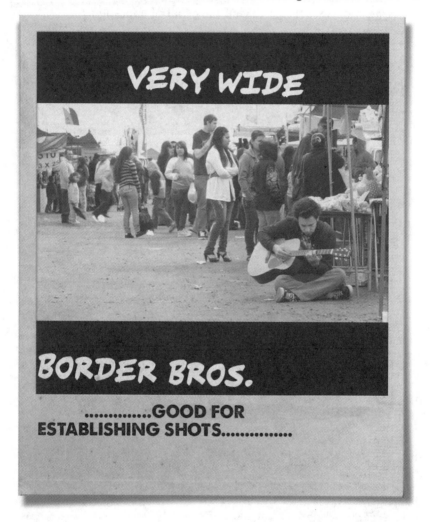

Wide Shot (WS). Good for action or displaying movement in scene.

Medium Shot (MS). The subject from the waist up.

Medium Close-Up (MCU). The halfway point between a medium shot and a close-up.

Close-Up (CU). Whether a glass of water or Norma Desmond, make sure your subject is in focus!

Extreme Close-Up (ECU). Often used for shots of eyes reacting to something, or waking up.

Over the Shoulder (OTS). Most commonly used during dialogue.

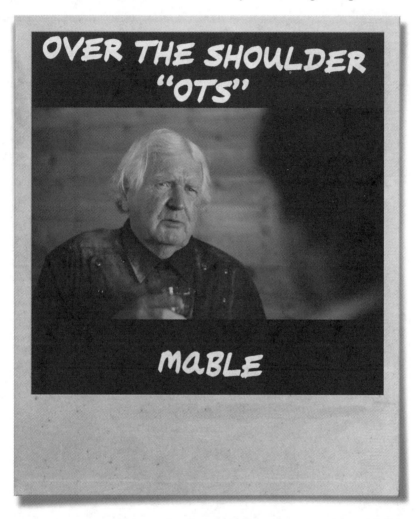

Point of View (POV). As if viewing from a character's eyes. These shots can be pretty fun to play around with. *Use sparingly.*

B-ROLL. EXTRA LOCATION FOOTAGE.
GREAT FOR CUTAWAYS THAT FURTHER
ESTABLISH LOCATION.

Chapter Eight

MONSTERS, GUNS, BLOOD. OH MY!

Special Effects, Makeup, and More...

This is the part of the book you don't tell your mom about. She'll complain that you're obsessed with monsters and violence, and we know that's totally true!

The truth is, special effects and special effects makeup can make or break a film. Whether your mom thinks you've gone over the deep end or not with your taste for violence and monsters, the last thing you want is someone calling you out on your big gun battle scene for looking too much like kids playing with sticks. No way! And that zombie head that's supposed to get sliced off? We can tell you made Mr. Undead's noggin out of Styrofoam. Not to mention the fake blood you're using looks like melted Crayola's.

Smh.

Now you're saying, "We'll just fix it in post!"

Rickey's Grandpa always did say, "Cheating's worth a good slap in the mouth."

Never fear! Not only will your face be free of red marks from Rickey's Grandpa, your gunfire and splatter scenes will be convincing movie fans of your movie-making prowess in no time.

Follow along for some of our favorite special effects tips. We'll talk about guns, blood, makeup, and even a little about monsters. While you're reading, watch for links to our very ripsniptious Cheap Movie Tricks special effects tutorials!

SPECIAL EFFECTS MAKEUP

Hey, was that you yelling outside our door? Uh oh, we hear you again...

"How do I get really great special effects makeup for my short film? Do I have to go to school?"

Come on, now. When did we ever say you had to go to film school?

"Then how am I gonna learn?"

You really don't have to ball-up on our front porch in a fetal position. For one, you don't have to learn special effects makeup at all. Your makeup artist can be someone you know who loves to do everybody's makeup during Halloween. It could be your best friend Zeke who says he's willing to watch YouTube special effects makeup tutorials. Or, maybe you know an actual makeup artist and you didn't realize it.

Of course, our recommendation would be to use a qualified special effects makeup artist. But as you know—they don't grow on trees— and they're not cheap.

With limited funds and limited access to such artists, there may not be a lot of choices. So do what you can. Just make sure your effects have an appearance of realism. No excuses.

SHOW LESS OF YOUR MONSTER

What kind of monster do you need for your film? Something little? Something big? Something demonic? Something cute with sharp teeth? Let's be real. Monsters range from deranged killers with bizarre body and facial features to giant hairy things that creep around like your uncle when he's sneaking up on the beer fridge.

Creating the scariest creature on Earth is difficult. What's even tougher is pulling off some sense of onscreen horror. Let's talk a little bit about shooting monsters for your film.

Many monsters may seem really creepy once they're built. It's difficult transferring that creepiness to the big screen. Well, that is until you read this book and learn how to literally turn those terrifying corners with your filmmaking.

Imagine watching a horror film. The killer sea monster is revealed and the camera lingers on this creature from the deep. But then a few seconds later you see through the veil. The creature is none other than Sam the Snorkeler wearing finger-paint makeup, *SpongeBob SquarePants* swim trunks, and kicking his way around a kiddy pool. Pretty crappy, huh?

But what if you can only afford Sam the Snorkeler? What do you do?

That's easy. Show less of the monster.

A Familiar Spirit

Try only showing your creature for a few seconds. Just like any good horror movie, less is always more, and if you need more, just add blood! In *A Familiar Spirit*, we cut our demon scenes to a bare minimum. Audience imaginations ran wild.

"What did I see?"

"What was that?"

Muahahaha.

We noticed in screenings the demon's creep factor shot through the roof. Don't forget, shadowy figures hide a lot of makeup flaws too. Always think creatively. And shoot test footage. Make sure your monster looks and feels real before you do take after take.

HOW TO BUILD A DEMON

So a zombie isn't your speed and you want to do a demon in your film. Let me tell you—with demons, less is better. More of a buildup will set the stage for bigger and better things. You can make your demon one of two ways. Either let your makeup artist come up with something, or you may be able to get a realistic looking mask off the Internet. You can also come up with some crazy concept art. Whatever you decide for the look will be *the* look. You need to get an idea of what you want the action to be like, too. Does this demon move fast or does it just stand there? How does it enter a room? To help your audience believe the demon is real, you need to make the demon do unnatural movements. This makes the movement as creepy as the makeup.

Lighting is also important when you reveal your beast. In our film *A Familiar Spirit*, every time we showcased the demon we tried to do some type of lighting adjustment, which made for some really cool demon shots that scared the crap outta people.

You may be thinking, "My demon looks crappy, but I still have to film!" Never fear, lack of lighting is here. Basically, you can dim the lights down. If it works in strip clubs to make the girls look better, why can't it make your demon look better, right? I haven't been in a lot of brightly lit bars... Get it? If you can't get the makeup you want, then only show bits and pieces. For example, showing just the hands, or maybe a quick shot of the eyes.

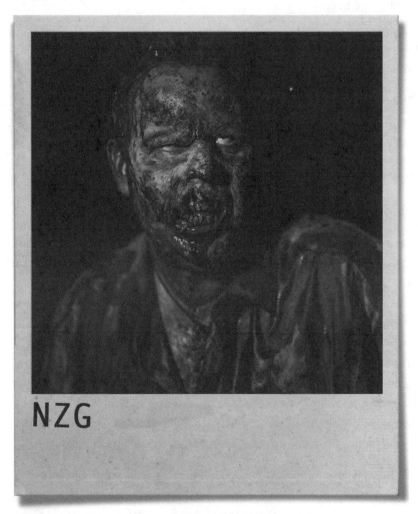

NZG

HOW TO BUILD A ZOMBIE

How do you build a zombie? Sure, you can have cool makeup and costumes, but it takes more. You have to think like the dead. You start the build by doing the makeup. Then you work on the clothes. Many times, people will have great makeup, but just clean clothes on their zombies. You need to think of the creature's back story. Where did she or he get killed? Maybe there was a struggle and the person's shirt ripped. Or if it has been a zombie for more than an hour, it's probably going to have blood on its hands. The little things like this make the difference.

Once your zombie is made up, you should start helping your actor get into character. They can act like they have pain when they walk. Or maybe drag their feet.

times, people will have great makeup, but just clean clothes on their

The most important part is to take away the human elements. Walking outta place or getting crazy quirks from your actors is a good start. Most importantly, have fun with the zombie characters.

Depending on what type of zombies you are doing really matters. Are they the Evil Dead or the Chemical Dead? Do they run fast or slow? You have to remember—in order to make the zombies believable, they need to be believable to you. Have your talent, aka zombie, break down to just their primal senses. The easiest way to make a zombie look good on camera is to have them fixate on something in the general direction of the camera and walk towards it. This makes the viewer feel like the zombie is looking at them and then moving forward towards them.

Just remember: keep you zombies bloody, dirty, and animated.

MONSTER SOUNDS AND MUSIC

The best way to make your monster creepy is to change the music. Think of Jason Voorhees or Freddy Kruger's calling music. Or even the loud shriek from Leatherface. It is important to give your monster a calling card. That way you can scare the audience without even seeing the monster. You have to remember that music helps with the emotions of your audience. Use that to your advantage. Make creepy music. David Lynch used random sounds in *Eraser Head* to build up the creepy elements to the film. Sounds and music will help scare your audience, or at least freak them out.

HOW ACTORS SHOULD INTERACT WITH MONSTERS

It is important to react appropriately towards a monster on screen. This is usually who your viewer will relate to emotion-wise. Think about it. If your talents' reaction to the monster is weak, you will deflate the intimidating presence the monster would have on screen. Even when your characters bring up or talk about the monster, there needs to be a type of fear. Your actors will help make your monster that much scarier.

Makeup camera testing

A lot of filmmakers worry about how good special effects makeup looks before the shoot. Are they shooting test footage? Sometimes they don't. Uh oh. Wasted time. Try a footage test. Fine tune how the creature appears on screen. Don't forget—the more blood the better.

BTS from "The Lackey"

SOME PROFESSIONAL TALK ABOUT GUNS

First off, are you a professional or an amateur? Trust us, you want to be considered a professional by your peers, whether this is your first or twentieth short film. You want to be the film studio everyone looks up to, the kind of movie professional others aspire to be. Such professionalism comes from you making killer short films, as well as talk on the street between actors and film crews about the respectability of your studio. You want respect, not laughter from the filmmaker scene. Got it? Good, then you'll take it to heart when we say, "Never use real guns of any kind on set." Keep a professional attitude about guns at all times. Don't let your actors or any unsupervised crew around such props. No horseplay either. Unprofessional behavior always leads to someone getting hurt, getting in trouble with the authorities, or both. So keep the real guns at home. Respect the weapon and your crew. You don't need anyone else around if you need a close-up of a real gun.

MAKING FAKE GUNS SEEM REAL

Fake guns can make your film shine with gangster toughness, secret-agent dazzle, and gritty realism. On the other hand, if you don't know what you're doing, your film will suffer. Filmmakers often lose sight of how guns should transform a scene. Too many times, actors wave guns around without anybody in the scene *reacting*. Is the character terrified of the weapon she's holding? Are other actor performances portraying characters scared out of their wits while seeing someone shooting a gun? Remember what we said about characters reacting to each other? Characters need to be in awe, or terrified, or completely petrified. Even strangely maniacal reactions to guns are *something*.

Other common mistakes pertain to the special effects side of the weapon: muzzle flashes and bullet hits. If you can't pull off a muzzle flash in post-production, then you're in trouble. You also don't want to use disappearing drag-and-drop blood bursts for bullet hits in your film.

So what should you buy? We recommend Airsoft guns that take CO2 and have blowback. These replica guns appear real and come in all types. Those with blowback seem like they're really discharging bullets, mimicking the kick of real weapons. Make sure to paint the orange tip of the gun. Grab some silver/metal modeling paint and put some age markings on the muzzle. This is good for close-ups and resembles a true gun. Remember what you see on set is not what your viewer will see. And there are lots of filters you can put on the scene to bring a sense of gritty realism.

Make sure you coach your actors to adjust to the light weight of the plastic gun. Real guns are much heavier. Also, don't get any footage of the gun hitting the ground. A plastic gun bounces. Super fake! You don't want that. Fixes include capturing footage of the gun sliding on the ground. You can also have your actor hold the gun while falling.

Limit your guns to those scenes necessary to move the story. Too many filmmakers have characters holding guns for no reason. Awkward!

Don't lose the onscreen power of a gun by showing one too soon.

GUNFIRE AND SPECIAL EFFECTS

You're watching a film. Gunfire breaks out onscreen. Everyone, including the little old granny in the film, is shooting like crazy. Problem is, nobody gets hit.

It may be okay for Hollywood to have every character immune to bullets. Not us.

You know the hipster in the back of the theater who says, "They should have reloaded the gun already"? We gotta be that guy. Do research on your fake gun. See how many bullets it can actually hold. When planning your scene, figure out where each bullet is going to hit.

Another issue is light. During editing, when a pre-set drag-and-drop muzzle flash is used, often editors don't consider how muzzle flashes should affect lighting. Let's say there are two gunshots from your character. Now, set up an off-camera light. You can use a bell light (shop light). Have one of your crew hang out by the light. Now grab your shot of the character holding the gun. Note: you may have to darken the scene a little for this to look really good.

How to use practical effects

Now you need to give a few practice gunshots. Flash the light for each shot. This creates light against your character and the background. See how the light appears to be coming from the muzzle flashes?

Now you need to worry about where the bullets are going to hit. Let's say one bullet hits a vase behind the character. Buy three identical glass vases from the dollar store. The thinner the glass, the better. Film the vase by itself. The next step is easy and fun. Grab a rubber band and make a little slingshot. Nothing crazy. You can even use your fingers to create the slingshot. Make sure important items are covered, including the camera and your eyes (also a good time to remind you to purchase goggles and safety glasses). Hit the record button. Now fire some small rocks with your sling shot at the vase. It should break and look like a bullet hit it. Note: Don't have breakable items or people in your line of sight while doing this.

How to film a good hit

"Where do I get muzzle flashes if I can't create them on my own?"

Oh yeah! Good question. We recommend VideoCopilot.com. Download muzzle flashes there. You can also purchase pre-sets that you can add in editing to make it appear that bullet shells are flying from the gun.

A MUZZLE FLASH

Time for the bullet hit! This has to look good. Unless you know someone certified in pyrotechnics, then you need to do this blood hit our way. So follow closely.

You need a tube, a confetti blaster, and some thick fake blood (more on blood in the next few pages).

All you need to do is connect the confetti blaster to the tube, then fill with blood. This is something you should try a few times before you actually start filming.

Oh, take precautions. There's potential here to get fake blood everywhere. So, you and the crew need to be wearing appropriate clothing. The confetti blaster is powered by a CO_2 cartridge. Buy a pack of those. It's best if the actor can control the blood blast. Depending on your budget, you may need to improvise. So what's about to happen? A quick force of air is going to push fake blood through the tube and through your actor's clothing. This can also be achieved by a paintball gun, or even an air compressor. So be creative and good luck!

Blood Gun Rig

Blood Hit Video

Hectic Films version of the guacamole gun

Our spin on a Robert Rodriquez gun invention is a rig that shoots blood and brains behind your zombie, human, alien, monster, or whatever. It's a really cool special effect that creates the illusion that a bullet passes through a head and splatters blood and brains on a wall. Here's our quick/cheap version:

You'll need the following:

- Fake blood
- Water bottle
- Sponge
- Really cheap paintball gun
- CO_2 cartridges
- Duct tape

Step one: Cut the bottom of the water bottle off. Next, use duct tape to attach the top of the water bottle to paintball gun.

Step two: Cut a piece of sponge. Dip it in fake blood. Stuff that piece in the barrel. This is your plug to keep fluid from entering the gun.

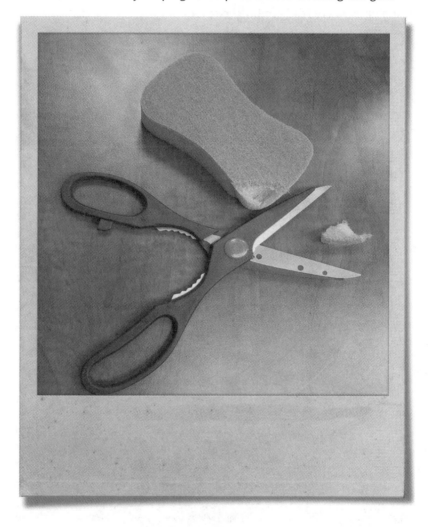

Step three: Add thick blood. If you want to use some salsa for brains, GO FOR IT! Just don't add too much or it won't work. Note: don't add blood until you're ready to hit the record button.

IF THE SPONGE IS TOO BRIGHT PAINT IT OR LET IT SOAK IN THE BLOOD

Step Four: Have your actor stand near a wall—the brains and blood have to hit somewhere! (The lighter color the wall, the better. And remember, you may not be able to clean off this blood, so do this somewhere you won't get in trouble or ruin anything that can't be splattered.) Have a crewmember with the blood gun between your actor and the wall. Once everyone is in place and the camera is ready to roll, add the blood into the gun. Have your actor react as if he was shot and have your gun blast at the same time. The blood should hit the wall in the general head area.

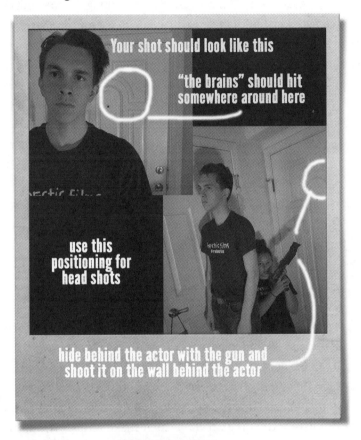

Guacamole Gun Video

THE BLOOD

Like gun prop faux pas, the improper use of blood can break a film. First thing we'd tell you is never say, "That's enough blood." Always take it one step higher. Remember, what you see on set doesn't translate the same to film. You have to make blood really stand out. Next, never dress your actors in dark clothing for a bloody scene. If you don't want to change the actor's clothes, that's okay. You can switch your blood rig to hit the wall, or just get creative. A final don't: no blood-filled scenes unless you have cleaning materials. Fake blood gets *everywhere*. We still have dried blood on a tripod from when we created a mess during our very first zombie movie shoot, *Wretched Flesh*. One of our biggest blood no-nos, we had to get the location carpets cleaned when we should have just laid down plastic. Cover stuff up and keep lots of baby wipes handy. Trust us, you'll need them.

FAKE BLOOD RECIPES

The easiest blood recipe is a bottle of Karo syrup mixed with a few drops of red and blue food coloring. Total cost should be under ten bucks. Try this: dump out a third of the syrup into a bowl. Set the bowl aside. Next, add eight to ten drops of red food coloring to the bottle. Then, add one to two drops of blue food coloring to the bottle. Top the bottle off with water then shake it up. If the bottle turns purple, you added too much blue and need to start over with a fresh bottle.

Thick Blood: Also made from Karo syrup. Great for close-ups and good for bullet hits. Also easier to shoot out of tubes and makes for realistic bleeding scenes. This type is also good for set dressing blood. You know, for when your cop character shows up to a bloody crime scene.

Blood Paint is exactly what you think. You can use anything from finger paint to watercolors. Your character getting beat up? This is the best way to keep some nice looking blood on his face. Fake blood by itself dries quickly and starts cracking. So, you'll have to paint a little stage blood over the painted blood so that it looks wet. Or you can use a little Vaseline over the blood spots (this trick also works to make your actor look sweaty). In some cases, fake blood will start turning green. Ack! Blood paint is also another good way to dress up a murder scene. Combining the thick blood and the paint blood makes for textured background gore. This type of blood is also good to keep continuity in your film. We used it to cover indie horror actress Meghan Chadeayne in *Naked Zombie Girl*.

For **Mouth Blood** order Zesty Mint Flavor Stage Blood from Ben Nye. It's about twelve dollars per bottle. Use the Nye blood so your actress/ actor won't be puking at the end of the scene. You'll get a better performance when the blood doesn't taste like dish soap and tomato juice. Yuck!

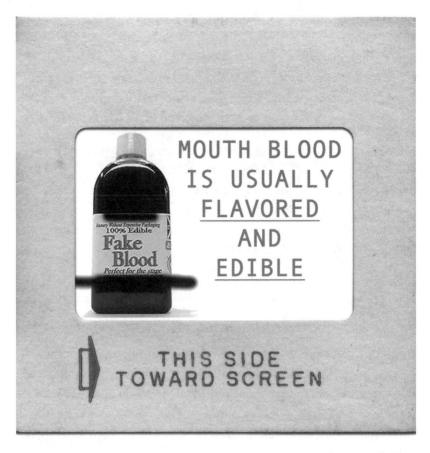

Sometimes consistency can be compromised and it's just easier to obtain a bunch of **Pig Blood**. Sissy Spacek was covered with it in the final scene of *Carrie*. Gross! We've heard of filmmakers going to butcher shops and requesting massive amounts of pig goo. Either way, if this is something that interests you, announce to your crew and actors what you plan to do way ahead of any filming, and make sure you don't use real blood in your blood rigs. Also, don't put it in anybody's' mouth. Disgusting!

Thin Blood should only be used when you need a lot at one time. Or use this in a spray bottle to squirt on the murderer's face while he cuts open his victim.

Punching 101

Hey, if someone gets socked in a movie, it better look good. Nothing worse than the *no-effort punch*. Whomp. Or the classic *punch towards the camera*. Oof! Don't ever punch at the camera unless you're shooting *Hardcore Henry* 2 (shot entirely in first-person POV). We mean it.

Your main character is being picked on and pushed around the entire film. Finally, he stands up to his bully. He goes to punch this guy in the face *Back to the Future* style (when Marty's dad hits Biff in the face). But it doesn't end up that way. You rush the punch scene and now the final cut looks like some crappy mime routine. It doesn't have to! You just need one of our Cheap Movie Tricks! (Lucky you.)

There are two people in the shot: the *hitter* and the *victim*. The victim will be facing away from the camera. Only his head and shoulder can be seen in the frame.

This is as close as you want to get when filming this type of scene. It's okay to get as wide as you want for your shot. You just want to be able to see the victim's reaction. You should leave an open space on the side of the frame so you're able to capture more movement. The hitter will need to face the camera with enough arm room to swing in front of the victim's face.

Punch in front of the
victim's face
crossing the camera

The hitter's swing should be in front of the victim. You want the swing flow from start to finish with no hesitation. You know how when you fake hit, you hesitate? You can't do that here. It needs to look real.

Move the camera slightly
with the punch

The victim needs to react in the same direction of the hit. To make it believable, stay in close on the shot; that way the victim can fall out of frame. If you want the wide shot, make sure the victim and the hitter stay in character. We wouldn't recommend staying on the shot long. A quick cut to show the victim's reaction is usually the best way to flow out of the shot.

The Indie Film Group

Need a place where you can go and watch countless films with stunts that you can examine? Try the Indie Film Group (theindiefilmgroup. com).

Chapter Nine

SHOOT DAYS

Your Mini Guide to Panic
Attack Prevention

If you're this far into your short film, you've come a long way.

Pat yourself on the back. You're making it happen!

Chances are you've had some frustrations along the way. Maybe even some panic attacks.

Don't worry. Every project has its setbacks.

driving shot in NZG

the cord broke so we had to wing it...

In *Naked Zombie Girl*, one of our sets was a three-wall shed. During filming, the shed kept blowing over. Winds practically tore it to pieces. Then the car we were filming our main character in broke down in the middle of a shoot. Can you believe we had to push that bucket up a hill just to make it look like it was running? Talk about improvising. If you look closely in the film you can actually see our shadows as we pushed the car off the road. Thank God for all those awesome crew members!

Think these frustrating moments only happen in indie movies? Think again. *Jaws'* main character—the shark in the movie—rarely ever worked while shooting. Did they throw their hands in the air and give up when Bruce was stalling in the water? Not at all. They got out of the mechanical great white what they needed: a terrifying shark! They made shit happen! Just like us pushing that bucket of bolts uphill just for a shot that we were determined to get! You gotta have courage—a fighting spirit—a don't-give-up attitude! You need to constantly move forward no matter if your set falls over in a windstorm, or your zombie head melts into goo. So let the hang-ups be what they are—mere creative hurdles. Not project killers. There's a way around everything. Remember that. Now how about some tips to help prevent you from your next potential meltdown?

GRAB THAT GOLD!

Your filming days are going to pass quicker than you realize. That means you've got to be a filmmaker on a mission during these few shoot days.

You've got to be on track to *grab the gold*!

The gold includes those breathtaking shots you don't quite expect to see when you suddenly outperform your planned storyboards. Or those moments that suddenly come when an actor's improvisation turns out to be something remarkable. Or when cinematography turns into beautiful and unexpected pieces of cinematic art. This is when your dedication to your project really shows. So instead of just being that robot who tries to get shots done in a timely fashion, be the filmmaker that takes a second before each shot to make sure everything feels right and looks great. Always be searching for something to make your shot even better. Be the filmmaker whose mind is open to unexpected moments of creativity. The film set can sometimes be a crazy war zone. You have to make sure your film doesn't reflect that.

Remember, always grab another shot after you think you have what you need. Don't go overboard and overshoot each scene, either. Just grab another take of the scene for peace of mind. This makes editing easier, because when you go back to look at the footage, you know the clip you need is always going to be there. Remember, this is not the part of the project where you settle for anything. This is the part of the project where you need to shine, where all your shot planning pays off.

DON'T FORGET YOUR SHOT LIST

One last reminder about your shot list: *don't forget it.* Make extra copies. Who would we be if we didn't remind you? This is one of your most important items as you shoot your film. If you mapped your list out right, then you should have all your bases covered. You'll be able to keep track of scene order, so double check, make sure everything is properly numbered/lettered before you start each shoot day. Keep extra copies of the shot list and your script. Things can get hectic on set, hence the name Hectic Films.

DAILY MEETINGS

Before filming, get together each shoot day for thirty minutes with your cast and crew. Go over everything. Explain the shots you'll be working on. Note any concerns regarding filming location. This helps mitigate some of the constant questions people will ask you while you're in the middle of a scene. There will still be those annoying random interruptions, so hold your cool and show patience. You're setting an example for future filmmakers. You can also appoint someone to be your assistant to help you with these issues (best idea ever). On the big sets, the Assistant Directors (Ads) run the show. Unfortunately, you don't always get such help when you're shooting on a budget. Maybe your neighbor who just wants to be involved will work for now.

PICK-UP SHOTS

You've finally reached the *martini shot* (the very last shot). It's not time to party just yet! Stop crying! Remember that shot you were supposed to get of the girl grabbing the knife off the table? Or that insert shot of the door handle getting grabbed? Tsk. Tsk. Pick-up shots aren't always wanted, but they always end up happening. These shots more often than not get missed in the grand scheme of things. This is the reason you have to stay on good terms with your location people. It makes it way easier to get these types of pick-ups.

Pick-up shot hacks

You know you need a pick-up shot of Julie seeing that zombie charging up the hill. You're kicking yourself. Ahh! You also need a bunch of other dumb punch-in type shots you missed of your characters grabbing things off a table, reaching in pockets, and locking the door as the zombies broke in to the house. Never fear! Here are some things to remember:

Once you start your project, have a meeting with your main actor/actress about no hair changes. No cutting or coloring for at least a month from the first day of shooting. This leaves you a better window of time to grab shots before the person changes their look.

Keep the clothes worn in the film for at least a month. That way you can do pick-up shots with the same clothes if need be. This also prevents that zombie actor from saying, "Oh man, I lost that shirt last week." Or, "It caught on fire!"

Remember, you don't always need pick-up shots for those actors whose face you don't see onscreen. That's why you have their clothes! Have someone else play the part!

Print out the shot you got for the scene you're grabbing the pick-up shot for. You need to match coloring and lighting.

Video/audio and marking your shots

You're going to be marking your shot in every scene. You can mark them on the chalkboard portion of your clapboard slate (clapper). You know that clappy thing that's really loud? Anyway, call out each scene number and take. Then slap that clapper! You should be using separate devices to record video and sound. Don't forget—you need to be able to easily sync clips. Best way to do this is to start audio and video at the same time. Once the sound operator is recording, she or he will call out, "Audio speeding!" That's when your Director of Photography (your cousin holding the camera) hits the record button on the camera and yells, "Camera speeding!" You then come in with your clapper and call out your scene number, shot angle (this will be on your shot list), the take number, and finally the clip number from the camera (should be located on the screen). The faster you say all this info the better. You'll thank us later when you get to editing this beast. Note: Never start filming a scene without doing this first. No exceptions.

Never "fix it in post"

Shooting your film is all-or-nothing! No cheating! No cutting corners. No praying for the gods to fix your script! (Way too late for that, anyway.) Unless you have a previously planned effect you're going to do later, never mutter the words, "We can just fix it in post!" It never works! So never do it! This will always come back and bite your butt harder than any hungry zombie could. If you can't get the shot, think of a work-around, or just cut the scene altogether. Make sure before you start cutting scenes that your story will still make sense without them. Think of this as going to the barber and asking for just a little off the top and then having that look of surprise when he brings out a straight razor. Just a little, okay? No need to lobotomize your film.

Chapter Ten

THE EXPERIENCE OF SENSORY DETAIL

In Other Words, Light and Sound

There's no other way to say this—and don't get disappointed—we hate when anyone feels like the whole world is against them. But who would we be if we weren't honest?

If your lighting and sound sucks, then your film is probably going to suck. And if your film sucks, then in your despair you might pizza binge to the point of explosion.

We've come *waaaaay* too far to let something like that happen.

We see you're getting the point—don't take lighting and sound lightly. Treat such movie magic with respect. In fact, *respect every aspect of your work and you're going to do great things.*

(We're pretty sure Rickey's Grandpa said this, too.)

We admit sound and lighting can be some of the most frustrating aspects of filmmaking. Both are time suckers during film shoots. Sound goes wonky. Bulbs break. Lights fall over. Sometimes shadows are just a huge pain in the ass.

Good thing you bought this book to get you through these hard times, right?

Keep reading...

LIGHTING

This isn't some high school production where flashlights and glow sticks are your friend. You need to professionally light your scenes in a way that looks and feels natural.

Got it?

Okay, maybe you still don't get it...

Look around. The lights are off. Sunlight is streaming into the room. See how the current light only brightens one side of Grandma's vase? That's natural lighting in a nutshell.

MAD SANTA -LIGHTING

take the time to
light

Movie lighting is more complex than just natural lighting, though. Making any scene feel believable depends on your own ability to illuminate objects and people while not over-brightening, or under-lighting. You have to experiment, to study up on techniques. Most of all, you have to get your hands dirty and start practicing at mimicking the different types of lighting we naturally see in our environments. Think about it, a jail cell is going to have much different lighting than that fancy restaurant dinner scene. Duh!

Three-Point Lighting Technique is the standard method used in visual media such as video, film, still photography, and computer-generated imagery. It's a simple but versatile system which forms the basis of most lighting. Once you understand three-point lighting, you're well on the way to properly illuminating every scene in your short film.

At Hectic Films we've added a few of our own modifications. Here's what we do:

Key Light is general lighting. You can brighten or dim this depending on the mood of the shot. Make sure your lights are dimmable. If not, you're using the wrong lights!

Second is *Fill Light*. This softer light should help kill all unwanted shadows and brighten selected people and/or items in the shot.

Third is *Source Light*. Knowing the source of illumination in your scene will help you determine how much brightness is needed. Is there a lamp on a table? Flickering neon signs and dim overhead lamps? Maybe a candle is brought into a dark room by one of the characters. Notice when this character enters how suddenly the entire area brightens. Lighting crews are on hand, slowly fading in more lights during these moments. But not too much—only a believable dimness, yet enough light is cast onto the characters to give the scene that vaguely familiar glow. Viewers are none the wiser because they're too focused on what the character is doing to start considering how much area that candle should be illuminating.

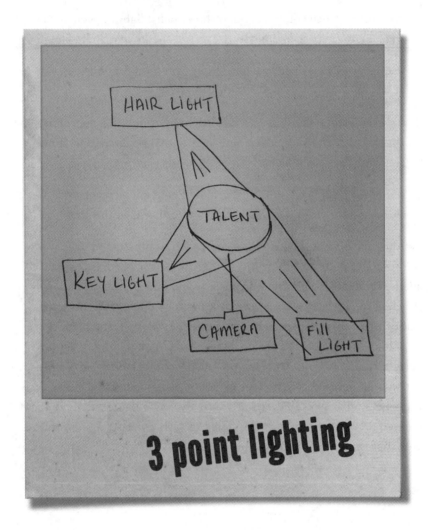

LIGHTING BLUNDERS

Hey, everybody messes up! Maybe you don't have to...

Don't use different colored temperature lights. This doesn't mean you can't add a little bit of red on your actors from that neon sign in your scene, but not to light your scene.

Remember, sometimes less is more. Adding too much light of any kind can cause everyone *and* your set to appear flat. Flat lighting makes your short film appear extremely low-budget. Part of your goal should be to look like you spent a hundred grand on your film, not the $2,000 we actually scraped up.

Don't allow lights to cast multiple shadows from your characters onto walls. This rookie move is a big no-no. We'll pull a soccer red card if you do, and you'll be ejected from the game! Got it? *No wall shadows.*

Also, don't light your characters from too low of an angle unless you're shooting someone telling scary stories around a campfire. This is unflattering lighting you want to avoid.

LIGHT LIKE THE PROS

No one can be as good as the pros, right?

Wrong.

fake source added

real source

When you light a scene think about where the light would be coming from

You're with us now. So listen up. There's an easy trick we use that makes people think we hired a highly paid gaffer (lighting guy).

Ready for this epic secret? You can't tell anyone about this.

Remember when we talked about making light look natural? All you need to do is light one side of your actor. Ha! Easy! Done! Look at that! *Au naturel!*

This cheap movie trick means you need to always consider where your light is coming from. As you move the camera, the lighting should match this technique in multiple shots. No cutting corners! Adjust your lighting with each shot. Keep your shadows on the opposite side of the light source.

SHOOTING IN DAYLIGHT

Shooting in daylight isn't all it's cracked up to be.

Consider the weather.

Seriously. You never know what crazy elements await.

Director Alfred Hitchcock said, "In documentary films God is the director." And that's because in documentary films, you're dealing with the real, and when you're outside, you have that real element of weather. Think about it. You can't control the sun. You can't control clouds. And you definitely can't control wind and rain. Until a filmmaker can make a deal with Mother Nature, you're just going to have to accept the reality that the weather isn't always your friend.

Here are some helpful hints as you battle the elements.

Your lead actress is about to give a Shakespearean monologue in your short film, *Awakening of the Damned*. She's squinting into the camera. You can't even tell the temperature of her skin tone. Lord Kelvin, where are you? (BTW, you need to search temperature charts. They're helpful and online).

There are tricks around your problem. The cheapest method (always our favorite) is to film indoors as much as possible.

Also, film in early morning or during the magic hour before sunset. Grab your shots quickly during nature's primo lighting. Keep in mind, lighting changes drastically every few minutes.

If you can't do a magic hour shoot, just promise us you won't film at noon when the sun is directly overhead. That's nature's worst lighting. Someone's nose will look like it's ten feet long in crappy lighting with those kind of shadows.

If you can, try to film in the shade. If there isn't any shade, create it yourself. You can do this with a *flag*. Ours is made of foam board from the dollar store that we taped together.

Now just shadow over your actor and voila! You just diffused the sun.

DOLLAR STORE LIGHT BOOSTS

Now that you've diffused the sun, you may need to use a little reflection to bring some light back on the scene. This part is easy. Just grab a reflective car window shade from the dollar store. You use these bad boys to capture the power of the sun and harness its power! You're shooting sunrays like an Egyptian god! Okay, you're just reflecting light, but still.

Reflecting light provides a beam or a streak. You can test this by experimenting how to reflect light onto a wall or a car (kinda like what you were doing earlier today with your cat and that laser pointer). Once you figure out how to find that light streak, move it onto your talent. Sometimes, on close-ups, you can let the actor hold it. It will brighten their shot. You can also reflect indoor lights this way too.

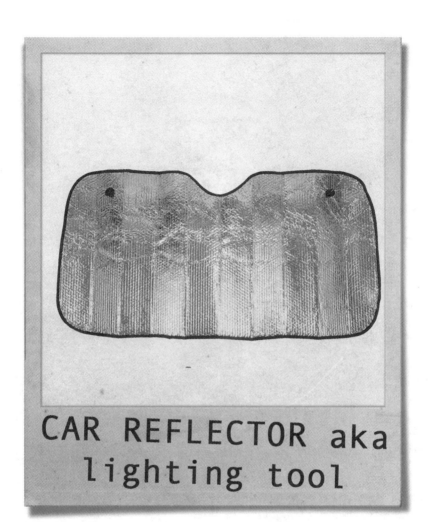

Make your own diffuser

Need to diffuse light? This trick will only cost a few bucks! Grab a shop light (bell light). Now you need wax paper. Last but not least, you need some C-47s. What are those? Clothespins. (Once you get on an actual movie set, the C-47s will somehow be a running joke. I don't know how this happens.) If you're in a pinch, a white sheet or even a white t-shirt can be used instead of wax paper. All you do is clip the wax paper to the edge of the shot light! No brain surgery required! If you need more diffusion, then just fold the wax paper in half.

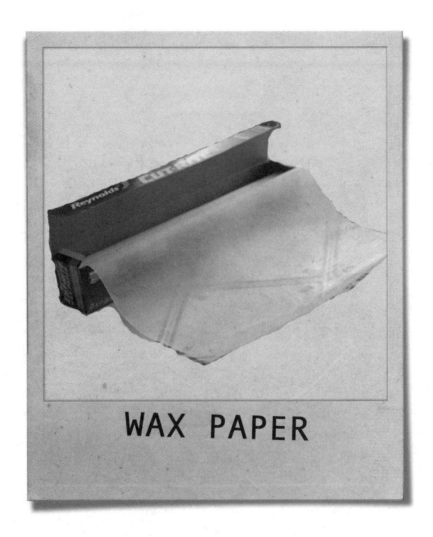

WAX PAPER

BELL LIGHT

BELL LIGHT

SOUND IS EVERYTHING

We don't need a hundred pages to tell you the importance of sound. Sound is everything! No one wants to return to the silent era. And no one wants to watch your crazy aunt playing her karaoke machine along to your short film (might be great for audience participation, but still!).

We already told you about using a secondary device (Zoom products) to capture audio. You still want to keep the camera mic on. This helps sync your clips. Never depend on just a camera mic for your main audio. Anyway, you need basics in capturing clean sound. You don't want static and hiccups. So let's do this cheap...

film slate

BACKGROUND NOISE

Background noise is the enemy. It's a huge pain in the you-know-what. It can be a guy mowing a lawn six houses down, loud exhaust from some jerk's car rolling through the streets, or that herd of yapping Chihuahuas you heard lived in the area. That's why it's better to film indoors—just saying. Don't worry. It's possible to obtain clean audio. Patience is the key. The trick is to have someone monitoring sound at all times to catch that quick dog bark or horn honk. Re-do the take. Otherwise you'll have a real problem in post. Strange how we don't hear certain sounds if we're not listening for them.

TRANSPARENCY

-JACK DOG-
*****HOME FREE

WIND INDOORS AND OUT

Wind is a sound killer. It doesn't have to be a huge windstorm for sound equipment to pick up that dreaded background hiss. It's important to get something like a *deadcat* wind muff (fury looking tail you put over the shotgun mic) to battle wind hiss. Rode has a mountable windshield called a *blimp*. Totally worth the money.

Sound killers also happen indoors. The static you hear could be the air conditioning. No brainer. Turn A/C off while filming. Shut it off while grabbing interior car shots, too. While filming our feature-length *Border Brothers* in the Mojave Desert, temperatures reached a hundred degrees. We don't know about you, but that's super-hot! There's a reason you don't see mermaids hitchhiking outside Vegas! But we're dedicated. We kept that car A/C off so we didn't spoil our clean audio. We all got a lot skinnier that day!

As The Man Drives
-jib shot

PLANES, TRAINS AND AUTOMOBILES — THE WILD TRACK

Sometimes the environment you're shooting in may just be loud. Too many squirrels arguing in the trees, or whatever. If that's the case, you need to make sure you record a *wild track*. That's thirty seconds to two minutes of location audio. The best way to do this is after you've finished your day's shoot. This audio track will be your best friend in post-production. Use this audio for piecing together smoother editing transitions.

Sound effects

Now that you have a recording device, start using it for sound effects! Have a door opening and closing in your scene? Grab an audio clip of that! Make sure you mark each special effect. At the beginning of the clip, name the sound effect (you should be naming all audio with scene and take numbers). Make sure you follow your actor grabbing the handle and shutting the door. You're a ghostbuster with a trap (your shotgun mic). The sound is the ghost! Go capture it!

Chapter Eleven

WHAT DID YOU
DO TO MY MOVIE?

How About a Crash Course
in Editing!

Editing is one of the most unappreciated jobs in the film industry. Watching hours and hours of footage, and then piecing together a sensible story. Legions of filmmakers have gone insane just staring at their monitors. Let's just say it's a process you have to love regardless of the pain and anxiety involved.

We've learned in editing that the shorter the final project, the better. Why? *Editing is your biggest roadblock.* Besides, today's audiences want their entertainment shorter and shorter. Whether or not we're all becoming numb and mindless and can't pay attention may be something you can explore in a film. For now, don't kill your back in the editing chair. Think about how you need to capture your audience in the first ten seconds, not the first ten minutes. So think strategically while you cut. And think about your audience. After all, you're making a film for them. Don't forget that. So constantly *trim the fat*. In the end, your final cut might be different from your script. Don't worry. What's most important is a short film that flows, that you love, and that looks good!

THE ORGANIZATION OF EDITING

The process will only get harder if you don't stay organized with your video and audio clips. Preview all clips and add to *scene folders*. In each scene folder, add audio and video folders. We put B-roll and establishing shots in their own folder. Make sure you're putting everything on your designated hard drive. Don't forget a secondary device to store back-up files of everything. Accidentally deleted footage or damaged hard drives could spell the end of your short film.

THE TIMELINE

While most editing programs are similar, we're going to focus on Adobe Premiere. In Adobe you have what's called a *Sequence*, or a *Timeline*. This is where you lay out all your video and make your cuts. It's simple once you get going. The most important function is the CRTL +Z, aka UNDO. Experiment with your functions but leave yourself a way out. You don't want to mess up and not be able to backtrack. If you want to get a little crazy with edits, we advise you to create a second sequence in the same project and experiment. Once you're close to being done with the project, you need to be careful. Changes can affect items on the timeline you didn't even know existed. Protect yourself and your project.

a Sequence or Time line
in Adobe

EDITING IN LAYERS

Many first-time editors hyper focus on one scene on their timeline. This type of editing process wastes hours. At Hectic Films, we *edit in layers*. No time wasting! We demand workflow! Place your best takes onto your timeline in order. Sync up sound as you go. Trim your project and get the timing in order. Make notes on what needs to be fixed or what pick-up shots are needed to make scenes make sense. Once you have a rough cut, start adding music. Next, add special effects, like muzzle flashes.

At this point, you can work on temperature and color. After you've color adjusted, then it's time for titling and video filters. Now, don't go insane. You're going to watch your rough cut a million times. It doesn't mean your audience will. So don't cut that awesome joke or epic death scene. You're probably overanalyzing. Ridley Scott once said, "When you're in the editing room, the dangerous thing is that it becomes like telling a joke again and again and again. Eventually, the joke starts to not be funny. So you have to be careful that you're not throwing the baby out with the bath water." So take a step back, let someone else watch the project. Don't give them disclaimers about issues—just let them watch it. See how they react. And listen to Ridley: *don't destroy your film*.

TRANSITIONS

Transitions can also make a film suffer. Too many page peels (a crappy transition) will make your film look like it was made by that uncle who loves *Flintstones* ringtones. The best transitions are dissolves and wipes. You can also do a straight cut with few or no transition effects. Our rule? Unless you're filming Adam West as *Batman*, then keep it simple.

SOUND SYNC / SOUND TRANSITIONS

You don't want your final cut to sound like a poorly-dubbed *Godzilla* flick. Programs like Red Giant's Pluraleyes will help sync audio to video. If that isn't in your budget, you'll need to sync the spikes yourself. This is where that pesky little clapper you've been using really comes in handy. You've marked each shot visually. The sound from your camera mic will show up as a spike in the timeline. In the audio you captured on your Zoom, your clapper shows up as a spike in the timeline, too. Sync those babies! Just don't put too many video clips together without getting your audio synced. Also, when blending audio, make sure you use fading audio transitions. Don't leave those harsh cuts in sound. This is where your *wild track* comes in handy. Place it beneath your sound transition. It should blend your audio nicely.

If your audio sucks and you know it needs to be fixed, save yourself a ton of headache and use Automated Dialog Replacement (ADR). Have your actors meet you at a sound studio where they'll be able to do the necessary voiceovers. It's important they're able to see the lines as they're being said on the film. Timing is everything when you're doing ADR.

A LITTLE MORE ABOUT SOUND

Once you've finished editing your film, make sure to review with noise-canceling headphones. Don't look at the film while you listen. Grab a notepad and review at least three times to make sure all your audio is correct and synced. Don't change anything right away. Just note the time stamps. For example, just write it like this: *Time 03:12: bad audio*. Once you've reviewed a few times, watch the film before making changes.

SOUND EFFECTS

Hey, Mr. Foley: make as many sound effects as you can (if you don't get this joke, look up what a foley is). After you've made a few films, you start to notice the same sound effects over and over again. You think all those judges at the film festivals don't notice five of the entries all have the same *cricket night sound*? There's only one re-usable sound we think is awesome: the Wilhelm Scream that has been used in over 225 movies. If you do want those free swoops and gunshot sounds, try Freesound.org.

Fruit can be brutal

Fruits and veggies can be used to create some awesome sounds. Celery and carrots sound like bones breaking. Squishing watermelon innards resembles a zombie eating guts. You get the idea. Now get to the farmer's market and bring back some sound effects!

Turn up the jams! Film music, score, and more...

Have you ever seen a movie with no soundtrack? Sucked, didn't it? We can't hate the silent film era. It was what it was. We've just grown accustomed to those eerie horror synth sounds when the killer is about to strike or the screeching violins during alien invasions. Heck, we need rock music in our contemporary road trips, and operatic concertos in our mega-fantasy flicks.

Music is simply a part of the feeling we all get while watching *anything*. Even your favorite YouTube star uses some kind of canned filler.

Star Wars needs its themes. One *Jaws* keystroke and you think a shark is up your ass. Better run!

Music transports us directly to film *mood*. It can be anything from an actual score or that one ditty from your buddy's band that will never see the light of day if not for your flick.

The point is—ask someone if you can use their music. Why not? Most local bands in your area aren't even trying to get signed. But they do need an outlet. Why not your film?

We wanted an eighties feel to *Naked Zombie Girl*. So we ran through the web and hit up bands whose songs we liked. Eighty percent were cool with us using their tracks. Those are good odds—so go with it!

Hollywood industry film studios have deep pockets as well as access to the who's who of the music industry. Price tags for those kinds of film music rights are way out of your budget and ours. We've used local bands in our projects, like The Silence Club, RVRBOY, and The Cretins. Remember all that talk about celebrities even on the local level and how using them can increase your fan base? This includes music. You never know when a band will help you promote. You might even win over some of their fans!

While contemporary music can serve the same purpose, *film score* has its own way of being built into scene structure. During production of *As the Man Drives*, we asked UK-based composer Tony Longworth if he would be interested in donating one of the film scores. He agreed. Talk about super awesome! Steven Castro scored the film's opening scene (also a donation). Thank you! Watch for these types of up-and-coming composers who simply need the experience. They're eager to work and really want to help. Another option is the *pre-existing score*. Those are usually the easiest to get for free. But they're not tailor-made to your script.

CORRECT THOSE COLORS!

Finished with your rough cut? Yes! It's time for another crash course from your friends at Cheap Movie Tricks. This time we're talking color corrections. You can't do them too soon or you'll create a mess. And you have to do them or your clips won't match.

Confused yet? Don't be. We'll just stick to basics.

In Adobe Premiere, locate the *Fast Color Corrector* by typing it into the search bar above your effects panel. Got it? Oh yeah!

You should have three colors to match: black, white, and grey. All you have to do is grab the *eyedropper icon* for each separate color. Match that color by clicking on the colors in your clip. For white, find the brightest white you can in your clip, and click on it with the dropper. Then find your darkest black with the black dropper and click on it. Do the same thing with that grey dropper. Just like a pro, you've done a quick color correction! Even if you're using filters, make sure you get all your color corrections done first. It will definitely affect your filters, and no one likes to backtrack.

VIDEO FILTERS

Projects can be ruined with filters. If they're too strong, you can lose clarity, color, and create a whole lot of visual noise and confusion. Beware of all the trendy filter gimmicks. You can easily be suckered into spending money that would be better spent on posters and Facebook ads.

We use Red Giant's Magic Bullet Looks. Check out their trial version. See if it works with what you want to accomplish. Don't waste money when you don't have to, right? The program's many presets will help you determine what look you want.

Green screen tricks

How about some green screen shots for some of those pick-ups? Let's do it! Just to keep it easy, leave the camera on the tripod for these (note: you can use a green screen in any type of shot. You can tape green on a fridge to add a flux capacitor in post!) Once you have your green screen set up, make sure you light the green screen evenly. That means no shadows. Also, no folds or wrinkles. Now add your actor(s). Don't place an actor too close to the green screen. This will cause that rookie green-screen reflection or bleed onto your actor. You know those cheesy used-car sales commercials with the green haze around the person? We don't want that. So light your character separate from your green screen. This also prevents your talent from looking blown out or overexposed. You can key out the green in After Effects or Premiere.

TITLING

If this is your first short film, keep your titles centered and simple. Don't use hard-to-read fonts like cursive or old English. That stuff looks tacky, anyway. Use bold text that stands out, something that complements your film. And don't hang on text too long. More than ten seconds is too long. A good rule of thumb is to read all the text then count to two. This gives your slower readers a shot at reading the message, too.

CREDIT SCROLLS

Before you set up your credits in Adobe Premiere, write them out on a spreadsheet. Open Office and Google have free spreadsheets! Who says technology isn't awesome? Once you've entered your info, select *title* in premiere. Then select the *scroll* option. Copy all your credits from your spreadsheet, pasting them in the *title box*. You can adjust how fast you want the text to scroll.

Chapter Twelve

YOUR MARKETING
MATTERS

Kick-Ass Movie Posters and
Other Artwork Tips

Presentation is everything—especially if you want other people to take you seriously. It's the same with any product, whether a soft drink or an advertisement for a new television show.

Let's get down to business: you need marketing that makes your short film stand out among the crowd. The first thing you need is a *kick-ass movie poster*. And we mean it, too. It really has to wow the crowd, fire them up, make them drool for the film it represents.

Your movie poster is what potential fans are going to see over and over again at film festivals, posted on walls, on flyers, on social media, and on IMDB, so it has to be great—it is the face of your product. Other than a movie trailer, this is your main selling tool.

We think you're getting the message.

But there's more...

Your poster has to be clean and professional. It has to be unique, incredible, and fit the genre of your film. You have to be competitive in design. You have to want to outdo all other film posters. The key is to make it look as catchy and professional as something you would see from a blockbuster theatrical release.

Assuming your layout skills aren't your strong suit, you need to hire a great artist. You need to be open-minded about their vision. The designer you're hiring is a professional. Let them do what they do best—design without you staring over their shoulder.

You can help them out by researching posters. Pick three simple designs. Remember: less is better. Not only is it a great design tip, it will mean the artist you're hiring is spending less time with your poster. And less time usually means less expensive (budget reminder No. 752). We've hired designers such as Dane Forst and Raul Gallardo. They never let us down.

**GREEN SCREEN SHOT FOR
THE NZG POSTER**

NAKED ZOMBIE GIRL

Naked Zombie Girl has gotten us into more festivals than any other film. However, with a great title comes great responsibility. We had to have a kick-ass movie poster. The real joke of the film was that through the whole movie you never saw actress Meghan Chadeayne completely nude. Even in the poster she's covered with the film title. That was Dane's idea. See? Listen to your designers. Let them create!

We did a quick photo shoot with photographer Robert Bejil for the image the designer used. Nick Reisinger did her makeup. You see? Even for a kick-ass movie poster, it takes a team effort!

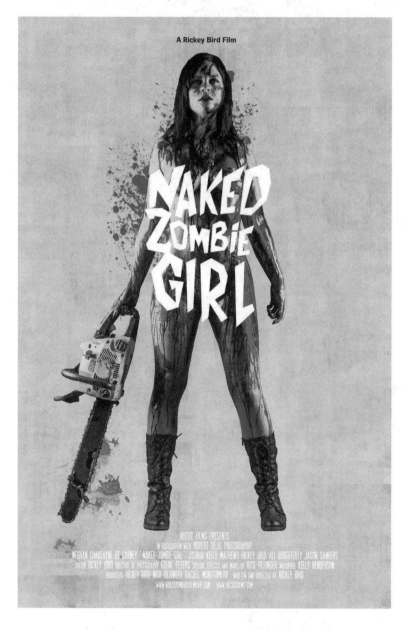

KEEP TO YOUR POSTER THEME

Now that you have a kick-ass movie poster design, you need to keep to the theme! Make it your header on its own Facebook page. Heck, if you have other Facebook pages, use it there, too. You can also use it on YouTube, e-newsletters, Twitter, and even that old MySpace account where only people locked in some kind of bizarre time loop lurk. Admit it, you still have an account (or your parents do). Start asking your crewmembers if they will add the poster design to their social media. But don't force them. We can't control each other's social media. And don't be mad if they don't. Either way, everyone will be seeing your poster image! In the short time *A Familiar Spirit* has been around, we've had a bazillion comments from people recognizing the demon on the poster. Not to mention, every event we've been to recently, we've included the demon artwork. Our posters get some mileage!

POSTER GIVEAWAY

Big poster sizes work great for screening. For our film *The Lackey*, we printed one large poster to put on the window of the theater. We normally give away 11x17 posters by the bucket load. Stick with that size. A nice glossy finish makes the poster professional. You can get a good price on PrintDirtCheap.com.. Don't plan on making a profit on posters. Use them for giveaways and promotions. Create a buzz about your short film!

POSTCARD PRINTS

Create postcard-sized designs of your kick-ass movie poster for film festivals. In your design, you need to include a blank spot you can later fill in festival information. You're going to lots of festivals, right? Then keep these handy!

Example: *We will be screening at _____ at _____. See you there!*

Hand them out at film festivals to get people excited about your screening. Hey, it's a competition. Just getting butts in seats can be a challenge. Don't forget to include an email address on your postcard. Something like (your short film title)@gmail.com. You never know who might try to contact you! This also prevents unwanted mail from your inbox. Step it up a notch and get an email from a web domain for your movie or film studio name!

ORIGINAL

#SCREAMFEST

table top at screamfest

MADE IN U.S.A.

BUSINESS CARD PRINTS

The easiest and cheapest way to market your film is with business card prints. They're super cheap! Online printing sites usually run their best deals with business cards. We, as indie guerilla filmmakers, use this to our advantage. Be as creative as you want! We print the poster of our latest film on the front. On the back we add a QR Scanner that links to either our site or a film trailer. That way, people can scan with their smartphones on the spot! You can literally have the QR go to a promotional video where you thank them for scanning the card and for watching the movie. But that's extra work. Don't forget to add your website URL to the card!

Chapter Thirteen

TIME FOR SOME
REEL TESTS!

Screenings and Promotions

Wipe away that sweat—you've done it!

Just don't look at your bank account.

Oh, drats. Hold the phone. You still have work to do.

None to worry! This is the fun part! You get to show off your project. Let's run some test screenings!

TEST SCREENINGS

Filmmakers need test screenings to gauge audience reaction. It's probably not a good idea to send out copies of your new awesome short film over your smartphone. You want real reactions, not half-answers from people squinting at their devices while they're in conversations with their friends over Facebook. The closer you can get your test screening to a movie experience, the better the results. So set up the biggest screen you can. The larger screens will also help the audience identify mistakes. If you don't have access to a theater or some kind of projector, you can hold your screening at Grandma's house with some people from the neighborhood, or against your buddy's garage using a rented projector. Either way, don't forget to encourage feedback. Provide questionnaires with ample room for comments. And bring pencils. Lots of them!

Make sure your audience is comprised of those who didn't work on your short film. In fact, the less your test audience knows about the story, the better. Though public criticism will sting after the screening, it's best to ask questions immediately after the screening.

Sample questions:

- "What was working for you?"
- "What wasn't working for you?"
- "What scenes would you cut?"
- "What storylines were too long?"
- "Which character stories were your favorite?"
- "Was anything redundant?"
- "Did anything not make sense?"
- "Was anything missing?"

IS IT A FILM PREMIERE OR A SCREENING EVENT?

Our strategy with movie premieres is simple. First, don't call them premieres. Call them *screening events*. This is because some festivals won't host your film if they know you've already had a premiere. Why? Because they want to premiere your film! Pretty cool, huh?

Maybe you're still thinking of showing your film in your hometown. Not a bad idea. Just don't spend your last remaining savings on a fancy theater. Why break the bank when you don't have to? We hold first showings at the cheapest venue we can find. That usually means the local dollar theater. You see, those big theaters normally charge by the seat. You can often rent a dollar theater for a flat rate. That usually adds up to being less expensive!

We held our first screening event for *Naked Zombie Girl* at a dollar theater. The screen was great, the theater was comfy, and the staff had fresh popcorn available in the lobby. We even had a red carpet and photo ops with our lead actress Meghan Chadeayne. We gave away a lot of posters that night.

If you're smart about your planning and can get people to come out, then your premiere can potentially rake in the money. This is good, because you need cash for the festival circuit (not to mention you have to budget for your next film!). But don't get mad if you don't rake in the dough. Be realistic. Any kind of marketing is tough. Just be glad that anyone comes to see your film at all.

Wherever you decide, make sure to plan at least two months in advance. This not only secures a venue, it allows ample time for marketing. You have to get tickets printed, press releases written. You'll need to explain key features regarding your films genre, runtime, and suggested rating. Submit your press releases to every type of news media in the area. From radio stations to podcasts, be diligent and persistent. Don't forget to set up all those social media posts. You got a lot of buzz to build. Get started!

THE SCREENING TRAILER

Film trailers have to be attention grabbers. Remember when we talked about story and we told you not to have boring, unoriginal material? Well, your trailer needs to be comprised of great material from your film. Don't build your trailer from the slow parts because you're too afraid to give away too much of your film. The audience needs to be teased with the story arc, and further teased with the film's conflict. But don't give away the entire plotline. And don't give away those monsters, either. You know how that ruins everything. Don't forget screening information at the end of your trailer. Also, the shorter the trailer, the better. Don't make it three minutes long when your film is only nine minutes. Aim for less than a minute. Online audiences are very picky and become disinterested really fast. Don't forget to upload your trailer to YouTube, Vimeo, and Facebook. Set up a schedule to share the trailer on different social media websites every few days. Get your view count up on all the platforms.

With Facebook promotion, you can target your audience and quickly see the results. Don't get too carried away by spamming the same post about your film over and over. Find creative ways to post the same information, and engage your audience in the comments. Be careful! It's very easy to overdo it on social media. When you do that, people will stop following you or just completely ignore your page.

Boost those facebook posts!

Boosted posts allow you to pay for exposure. Your page follows will increase once you do! When creating the boosted post audience for *Naked Zombie Girl*, we added every zombie movie imaginable because of the movie comparison you can do in the boost post. This is how you can single out your fan base! Just because someone likes zombie movies doesn't mean he will love your zombie movie, but at least you know the people liking your post/page are people who like zombie movies! You can spend as low as a dollar a day to help the promotional process.

STOP COMPLAINING—GET TO WORK PROMOTING

Quit complaining how poorly your social media is doing. You have no content! Barely any description on the pages no links, no videos, no pictures. We live in a digital age. More and more people are constantly on the web. With smartphones people spend a lot of time on the web. I used to get mad when a bunch of people would call me asking me dumb questions about the film. Then I realized I wasn't putting this information anywhere for people to find, and by not taking the time to get all the information out there, I would be screwing myself. Not only myself, but then when someone is trying to do a write-up about us, they do not get all the info. That's when you start losing out completely. So Rickey came up with the Hectic Films Top 6 promotional checklist.

SOCIAL MEDIA - Make sure you have an account for your short film on all the major social media platforms. Make sure each account has all the information needed for the film. There may be some facts you have to update later; just make sure you do it to all of them. They must have the following: poster for the film, cast photos, screen grabs from the film, and the film trailer (if there isn't a way to upload your trailer, just paste a link to it from YouTube). You should also include what the film is about, casting and crew information, and lastly, the website. Keep your names on social media just the film name. It makes it the easiest. Please note that you need to start these accounts before you start crowd funding.

PRESS RELEASES – Make sure you have a general press release for your film. Just for the film. Include the trailer links, the poster, and some shot from the film. Explain yourself and your film and any key elements in the film that make it stand out and make it different. Once the press release is finished, upload it to as many places as you can find. Also, keep a copy of it on your film's website, labeled under Press Releases. Then once you get on your film festival tour, you should create a press release for each time it screens at a fest.

WEBSITE – Your website home page should be basic, like just displaying the trailer of the film so it is the first thing people see when they go on your site. You can create a site on your own with site builder from GoDaddy, or you can do a little research and create a WordPress site on your own. Either way you go, the way you DO NOT go is getting a free website service. This is too cheap. Spend the fourteen bucks and get the domain at least if you are struggling to get the coin to pay for a year of hosting. Again something you can start an Indiegogo or GoFundMe for. Make sure you add the following tabs: Info, Contact Us, Screening Dates, Press Releases, Blog, Social Media. You can add more tabs, but these are the mandatory ones needed to have a strong online presence.

IMDB — The Internet Movie Data Base is something that a lot of people use in the industry. You need to get your film on here. If you do not have any prior credits, it takes a little extra work. Make sure you have all your social media sites done before creating your IMDB page. That way, they have something to reference. Once you have your IMDB page, you have your street credit. Well, the start of it. It would kinda be like starting a new shooter game at level two.

BLOG — A blog is where you can write about your day on set or anything that is related to the film. This should be where you post updates for your film as well. Once you post on your blog, you need to share the link to the blog post on all your social media accounts. This drives people to your blog/site and it makes it easier to share over multiple platforms. There are a TON of blog type services; one free one we use is Blogger. You can use whatever you want. So, write a blog share on multiple social media platforms. Got it? If you can't write a blog, just upload some pictures from set.

YOU NEED A HASHTAG!

This old man used to say "a closed mouth doesn't get fed." How true that is in all things film. Now, we're not saying to keep yelling; what we are saying is to get out there and ask people to like your pages. Once they like your page or follow you, you need to remind them to share with others. So instead of just posting, "Look at us on set!" on social media, post something like this:

Look at us on set! Please go check out our trailer!

(Post a link to the trailer)

Please like, comment, and share! Thank you! #yourhashtag

It is important to include additional information on your posts and always include your hashtag.

REVIEWS

Reviews help get your film out to the masses. We contacted horror sites for reviews of *A Familiar Spirit*. We posted those on our site. Content! Hooray!

The best way to approach film news sites and blogs is to include your press release, poster, and a link to view the film via a private link. If you're worried someone is going to steal your film, add a watermark. Or just be super careful where you send your films. Either way, when someone reviews your short film on social media or just on blogs, it will help your project get some attention. Their fans will hopefully look at your work, and you need to save those links to store on your film's website. Use it as a list to reach out to those people to review your next film. This also helps your social media sites and gives you a reason to post. Don't let a bad review get you down. Sometimes the bad reviews are good for you later. It will help you take a different look at your film and possibly improve it.

Chapter Fourteen

FILM FESTIVALS

Film festivals can be tricky if you don't use your common sense. Our Western short film *Mable* wouldn't do too well at a horror festival. No brainer, right?

What if there's a horror film festival you really want to get your thriller into? Do you really want to take that chance? Most any thriller makes for weak horror. It doesn't fit the theme. And that's a waste of time and money. There are film festivals happy to accept films of every genre. Some are expensive. Others are rip-offs.

We've said it before—the best way to submit your film to festivals is through FilmFreeway.com. Fill out all the information on the site for new members then upload your short film to Vimeo.com. Use the private link to showcase your film on the site. You'll find lots of free festivals. Submit only to the categories that fit your film's genre.

Make sure to upload pictures and any reviews you've listed. Once all your info is complete, you can browse festivals and submit to festivals. Another film festival submission website is Withoutabox.com. The site isn't as user friendly, but don't scrub them off your list—you might find a great film festival through them.

WHAT TO LOOK FOR

Discover a potential film festival? Good. Start doing some research. Why? It still might not fit what you're searching for as a showcase for your film. Check out their Facebook page and website. What are they promoting? Products? A library? Christian only? Teen films only? Latinos only? Is their festival only for filmmakers who live in Florida? How many likes on Facebook do they actually have? What's the cost of their festival? Look, you don't want to be screwed out of money by submitting to a tiny one-time festival in a library that time forgot in a corner of the world no one knows about. The real kicker is festival attendance. How many people go to this thing? A thousand rabid horror fans? A couple of dudes screening cartoons in their basement for the five idiots dumb enough to send them money? Avoid the weirdos.

You might want to only submit to festivals that you can actually attend. Which festivals land within a two-hundred-mile radius? What major cities are in your area? Which nearby festivals are the cheapest? Can you afford a few cheap festivals and one of the larger ones? Be strategic. Most festivals get more expensive the closer it gets to their event dates, so the earlier you submit, the better. Early bird specials are the way to go.

THE FEST

You've made some decisions. You've submitted to three festivals. *Zombies Taste Like Broccoli* got accepted to two. Way to go! You're even able to attend.

Now that you've arrived, let's go over some strategies and dangers...

POSITIVE STRATEGIES

- Look and act professional.
- Bring business cards and DVDs of your film (include your email and film title).
- Find the event organizer (festival founder). Thank them for accepting your film.
- Stay as long as you can to support the fest. Watch at least three films that aren't your own. Leaving early is a crummy thing to do.
- Buy a program or t-shirt to support the fest.
- Pass out those postcards with your film's screening time.
- Take lots of photos!
- Constantly post updates to your social media networks.
- Take notes about films and stay positive.

NO NEGATIVITY

- Don't talk badly to anyone, or about any films.
- Don't post negative comments about the festival.
- Trash talking is not cool.
- Do not only watch your film.
- Don't be a jerk if things don't work out for you.
- Don't demand the festival do things for you during your screening.

FESTIVAL AWARDS

Awards are great to get. But if your film wasn't chosen, just swallow your pride. You'll learn from your experience, make another film, and win next time. And you never know, one festival you might lose, another you might win. The reality is winning takes time. In the meantime, be glad you made it into their festival. You'll still get a set of laurels to place on your poster for being an official selection. Don't put too much credence on small festival awards, anyway. Don't get us wrong—it's a blessing to win *anything*. But winning awards isn't going to magically turn your short film into a feature, or cause money to fall from the sky. Turning a short film into a feature comes from creating an awesome film, networking with potential producers, showcasing your film at reputable festivals, raising cash, and a lot of luck.

The best way to turn your short film into a feature is to use your short film as the pitch for your feature, especially if you make a good short film and have a feature script alongside it. Every recognition from film festivals will just increase your chances of getting your film made into a feature.

Chapter Fifteen

GETTING A
FEATURE DEAL

Well, this is why we are doing this, right? If you are reading this, then it means you finished the FILM!!! Congrats! You made it. Pat yourself on the back. Write down a list of the people who said you couldn't do it and give them a call to make sure they know you did. Then don't forget the people who helped you get the film done as well. Take time to thank them personally; after all; they helped you get here. Also remember this film is not just *your* film now. So when you refer to the film, say things like, "our film" or, "we did this or that." Without these people, you would not have a film. Remember that.

Getting a feature deal could easily depend on the quality of your project. It could also depend on what film festivals you submit to. It can greatly depend what you do with the project. If you think you have GOLD and you want to get the film into Sundance, GO FOR IT. If you want to go more of the high class route, then only enter in a few upscale festivals. This is what we like to call a lottery strategy, because even if your work is good, sometimes it's just the luck of the draw. A lot of time, people say, "You can make it in those fests, I have seen way worse films in them." Usually the case is, if the film sucks and is still in the fest, then they have an "in," aka they know someone important or have ties to the fest. Do not compare yourself to people that already have a shoe in the industry.

If you want to get into a bigger fest, watch some of the short films from the festivals previous year. If your short isn't in the same league, don't worry... most of those people shoot films for thousands of dollars. I was in a fest in Austin, Texas called the Austin Revolution Festival, and no one could believe that I shot our film *As the Man Drives* for under $400 and was competing against films that had actors with higher day rates than the whole budget of our film. The point is, if you put your short into a large well-known fest, you can slim your chances of getting interest in your film.

FILM FESTIVAL DISTRIBUTION DEALS

These rarely happen, so don't plan on it. It can still happen, but so can meteors hitting planet Earth. The days of walking into a fest with a film and walking out with a distribution deal died in the '90s, although most "indie film books" will tell you differently. Usually the festivals are full of people promoting their film project, so they are not really looking to fund feature deals from random filmmakers. Again, not to say this doesn't happen, it's just foolish to think that you would be able to make a deal here. You need to use these festivals to create value in your project. As soon as your film wins awards, you need to add these to IMDB and your website. Then you can start referring to your film as an award-winning film. Has a nice ring to it, doesn't it?

PACKAGE YOUR FEATURE SCRIPT – FROM YOUR SHORT

Your short film will be a piece of your marketing material for your feature film. If you want to do another feature not based off your short film, it may be a little harder to get something like that off the ground. You can also do an anthology of three or more short films. Either way, you need to make sure you have the following: a script, a synopsis of the film, and a rough budget. The key is to get a realistic budget of what you will need to pull it off based on a five–to-eight-page-a-day shooting schedule. How many days did it take you to film that short film? How many pages of script did you shoot per day? You need to make sure you keep track of these to give yourself a rough estimate of how much you need to make a feature from your short film. Especially since you have no money to pay someone to do it! Then you should already have a poster and a trailer for your short. You can use these for your feature, and now it keeps the value of all your hard work from your short film into your feature.

SELF-DISTRIBITION

This may not be the best way to go with your short film, but if you take the time to advertise, you can use sites like VHX.com to grab a profit from your film. There are a lot of different self-distribution outlets on the web. Even Amazon will give you an option to actually sell a DVD through CreateSpace.com. The only problem with this route is you may have to invest in some advertising to get the word out about your film. So, the same type of strategy will be needed to promote your film being for sale. The more you push your film, the more sales you can get. However, unless you have a name actor in the film, people may not give you their money to see a short film. If this is the case, just upload your film on as many different platforms as possible for people to watch and help get your name and your film out there.

THINGS TO REMEMBER WHEN SIGNING A DEAL

The hardest lesson I learned in the filmmaking business was funding my first film *Phase Two*. I didn't read the contract correctly and paid dearly for it. Our script was pulled apart and changed around for very dumb reasons. We had no control. From this tragedy, I learned a lesson about contracts. Never give up your creative rights to the film. If it is not addressed in the contract, then you would need to get something on there that says it will be.

Another thing to understand is if it is a non-exclusive agreement. What's a non-exclusive agreement?

Non-exclusive contracts allow a second party to publish or distribute intellectual or creative work, but it does not prohibit the owner of the work from selling her work to other vendors.

How to package a film, from our friends
John Blythe and Myron Ward

For packaging a film, you should first start with a project that has marketable appeal. Once a script is completed and the essential players (director and producer) are involved, seek out a reputable agency that can work with you to secure talent, either through a letter of intent or direct attachment to the film. It will take some money to secure attachments, but this is where the second step comes in hand, which is financing, and this is perhaps the most crucial to getting your film into production and at times the most difficult. Once a budget is finalized, there are different approaches to film finance, such as equity, lender and gap financing, international co-productions, state tax incentive programs, and pre-sales. Sometimes to finance one film can be a combination of all of these finance structures.

For independent filmmaking, the most common approach is private equity financing. Rule #1, a filmmaker should never use his or her own money; always use other people's money who can afford the risk, but please be sure to spell out the risks and understand the laws concerning financing. The next step is getting the film into physical production and post-production, which is usually around two to three months average. Make sure to find good locations that can make your film look ten times better and utilize crews that can work well together and help you bring your project into fruition. A good line producer and UPM can be instrumental in making sure the film is on schedule and within budget. Finally, distribution is important, because this is where revenue flows in to allow a good return on investment and hopefully allow the filmmaker to earn income as well. Distribution delivery schedules are always lengthy. Make sure you have all of the necessary items to deliver to a distributor; negotiate an advance to help offset some of the costs associated with the schedule and try to negotiate a cap on the P&A (prints and advertising) budget expense, because this is recoupable cost. Good contract negotiating will help make sure the film is successful financially.

The Bonus Chapter

HOW TO FILM A
KILL SCENE

There are a lot of seasoned filmmakers that struggle with this. So we give you this info to make you money shots, aka THE KILL SCENES. This is the most important part of the film; if a scene like this is included in your script, you want to make it good... really good. So good that people will remember it. Here are a few insider tips on how to make an EPIC KILL SCENE:

First, you need to come up with your kill. For the sake of an example, we will use the classic Alfred Hitchcock film *Psycho*. Just in case you haven't seen it, there is a famous kill scene where Norman Bates kills Marion Crane in the shower. You should look it up on YouTube if you haven't seen it, but there are some really great elements in this scene. First is Marion gets murdered in the shower completely naked. However, we see no nudity. The second element is that we never even see the knife enter Marion's body. Think about it. We have a naked woman that gets killed in the shower and we never see anything. Could you image Alfred Hitchcock trying to pitch that part of the movie? Yeah, I want to film a naked woman getting stabbed in a shower... Sure that went over well in 1959-1960, but Alfred did it and made history while doing so. There are five important items that make up a good kill scene. Lucky for you we are gonna share them with ya!

The Weapon. What kind of weapon are you going to use? A knife? A crowbar? A rope? The weapon is the important part of the kill scene. No matter what the weapon is, you should still treat the knife as a character. Make a shot where the weapon is displayed by itself on its own. Give the thing its close-ups. Why? Think about if someone pulled a weapon out to hurt you. Would you be looking at the person's feet, or would you be looking at the weapon and possibly their face? So you need these exclusive types of shots in your film. These types of shots put your audience in the victim's shoes, making the kill scene more impactful. Also figuring out what weapon you are going to use and how the kill will work is very important. And you need to have a fake version of the weapon. It's okay to show a real knife in a close-up, but not okay to use the real knife for stunts or the actual kill scene in the film. After all, you don't wanna film a real murder, right? Once your audience see the murder weapon in a close-up shot, you could honestly use a nerf gun bullet in its place on a wide shot and your audience won't be able to tell.

The Acting. This is another important part of the kill scene. We can go on for roughly three days on this topic, but we will try and keep it to the point. Bad acting will weaken your kill scene and maybe make people not want to watch the rest of the film. The odds that you will be working with inexperienced talent are pretty high in the indie film world. Never fear, we have your back! The first scenario would be you have a person that can act. You want to make sure you grab some closes ups on your talent. First couple of shots needs to be close-ups on their face in pure fear. Depending on the character and the setting, aka location, it may vary on how much range you are wanting in the scene from the talent. For example, if the dude is a tough guy, then maybe he won't shriek at the top of his lungs when he sees the killer. However, some element of fear from the talent is crucial to get across the danger to the character in your story. Once you grab those close-ups, the next thing you should work on is the kill itself. How is your talent re-acting the knife blow? Does it look real? If you have a really good actress/actor, then this will be easy. If you have someone that may be struggling, then you won't want to show too much of your victim. Which leads us to our second scenario—where your talent can't seem to pull off the shot. This is actually easier than you would think. Get your shot set up with the talent. Then hit the record button as if you are getting some test footage. Have someone on your crew put on a mask and hide. Don't tell your talent. Now, you shouldn't jump out and scare your actor unless it's needed. The best way is to have the person with the mask on come into the scene off-camera (in the general direction where the killer would be standing off-camera). If you do not acknowledge the person in the mask, it gives you a creepy vibe from your talent. If that doesn't work, usually an over the shoulder type of look off camera is the best way. This is where you start the scene with your talent looking down or off to the side, then "hears" something and looks in the general direction of camera but eyes still off to the side looking at the killer. The other "cheat" would be to be creative with your camera angles. Another trick during the death scene would be to show the victim's hand as it hits the ground, or film from the back of the victim. So if your talent can act, use that to help sell the scene; if your talent can't really act, then get creative with either scaring the reaction out of them or getting creative with angles that do not showcase the person's face.

Sounds and Music. This is yet another element to kill scenes that do not get enough credit. You need to let these scenes "breathe," aka give it some time to buildup. This is where that creepy buildup music comes from. You know the real reason you feared Jaws wasn't actually seeing the shark, but that scary buildup music. So think about that when you start the scene. Maybe the camera creeps down a dark hallway with the only light on at the end of the hall: the room with the victim. Toss in a little creepy buildup music and you have yourself a scene! The other element here is the sound. The sound is really important. It is another part of the "hook" to grab your audience into the scene. The issue here with a lot of filmmakers is that they don't spend enough time grabbing the right sounds. When the knife hits the victim there should be gruesome sounds of blood and impact. Make your audience feel every single stab or hit.

The SFX, aka The Special Effects. Practical "in camera" effects are usually the best option for the indie filmmaker on a tight budget and still make it believable to your audience. One mistake made by a lot of new filmmakers is not doing their special effects correctly or letting the camera linger on poor special effects. You don't want to do this. So if you stab someone in your film, you can't just get a small amount of blood coming out of their mouth. You need to get it bloody. The good thing about fake blood is it is CHEAP. You can make a bunch of it for a decent price. So if someone in your film gets stabbed, then you need to use lots of blood. All you need is a little Karo syrup and blue and red food coloring to make the blood. Let's say you are somewhere you can't get the floor bloody. Then you would grab a shot of the ground somewhere that is cool to get blood on it. Remember, the audience only sees what you allow the camera to see. Or you can change the place in which the kill happens. Make it happen in a bathtub or outside. Places where you know you can get a little messy may be a better course of action. If you want to show the actual penetration of the murder weapon, do so on a tight shot, meaning only show the point of entry and some blood. Don't stay on these types of shots for more than ten seconds in your final edit.

The Editing. Last but not least, THE EDITING! Editing is another huge element. No, we are not going to give the secret of L and J cuts in Adobe. We are just going to help give you the necessary editing choices you need to make to create a powerful kill scene. Because if you don't edit the kill scene correctly, it will look like CRAP. Nobody came to see a turd—they came to see some blood! So, how do you keep your kill scene from looking bad? Well, you do it by giving yourself the proper "buildup". If you made your characters somewhat likable, then the audience should care if they get killed. So the buildup is important to get your audience set up for a murder. You know when you're watching a movie before someone is going to get murdered? The music changes and we usually see an unsuspecting victim. These are all elements to a good kill scene. Don't rush into it. Give your audience time to develop their own sense of danger. Then, when you edit the actual kill scene, you make sure it stays believable. What do we mean by this? Make sure every shot that you choose is a convincing one. If it's not, then cut the shot. Victim starts to smile as they get stabbed? CUT IT! In a kill scene, less is always more. Always. Make sure you also include a good shot of the murder weapon so the audience can clearly see the weapon. Get a solid, aka really good, take of your victim's response. Sometimes it's better to show the victim's reaction to the killer before they get killed, but that really depends on your actress or actor. Can they give a believable performance? If they can't, then show them in more of an obscure style shot, possibly leaving them out of focus, or move the camera further from the talent. This will hide the acting flaws.

DEAR FILMMAKER,

You are probably like me. You want to make movies but have no money to make it happen. Making a film isn't as simple as most forms of art. It takes a team. It's a very difficult process that not many can do. Though many have been in this same position, saying, "I wanna be a filmmaker," many never get past that point. Once they dive into a film project, they find out that it isn't easy as it seems. They give up. Not you. You can't give up. Filmmakers are storytellers. And storytellers need to tell stories. It's not always going to be easy, but I can tell you from years of making films on extremely limited budgets: I wouldn't want to do anything else. That's why we wanted to create a book to help someone just like you. I am no different and was in your shoes at the starting line of my career. I had to get extra jobs, stay up late at night. When you don't have a foot in the door, sometimes it makes it harder to open. That only means one thing. You will appreciate it when you get to the other side of the door.

If you want be a filmmaker, you need to make sure that you are committed not only to your film, but to your talent and crew. No matter if they show up for one day and barely do anything. They were and are a part of the project. Remember, when you make a film, you are the captain of that ship. Not only does the captain go down with the ship, but the captain has an important role in crew morale. So stay positive and it will be contagious. You have to be a glass-is-half-full type of person even if your camera catches on fire.

No matter what the issue, keep going forward with your film and continue to stay positive. Don't let negativity control your filmmaking path. Sometimes it's not only the elements, but flaky people bailing out that can cause problems. So never think that your problems with your film are too big to conquer. Just figure out an actual solution and solve it. Remember that it is not only your hard work, it's also all the hard work from the people that helped you. Just keep making movies, much love.

—Rickey Bird Jr.

P.S.

This book is not going to make you a master at one element of production, like a master editor. What it will do is give you an overview and enough knowledge to give you the understanding of each process so that you can take charge of your project and become a master filmmaker.

RICKEY WITH
KEVIN SMITH